a Consumer Publication

THE LEGAL SIDE OF BUYING A HOUSE

Consumers' Association
Publishers of **Which?**
14 Buckingham Street
London WC2N 6DS

a Consumer Publication

edited by Edith Rudinger

published by Consumers' Association
publishers of **Which?**

Consumer publications are available from Consumers'
Association and from booksellers. Details of other
Consumer Publications are given at the end of this
book.

ISBN 0 85202 112 7

Computer type-set by
Page Bros (Norwich) Ltd

The buyer and the seller may wonder exactly what part solicitors play in the transfer of a house. There is widespread misunderstanding about what solicitors have to do when houses are bought and sold; many people seriously underestimate the amount of the solicitors' work, and the responsibility they take.

Conveyancing covers a very wide range of activities, from the intricacies of trust law to the niceties of redevelopment in city centres. This book presents a picture of conveyancing at its very simplest, but at the same time one that affects thousands of individual consumers every year: the typical transfer of a house in England or Wales, wholly occupied by the seller, and with a title which is already registered.

THE LEGAL SIDE OF BUYING A HOUSE explains step by step the procedure on transferring such a house. A detailed explanation is given of the functions of the solicitors acting for the buyer, the seller and the building society. The parts played by the estate agent, the surveyor, the Land Registry, the insurance company and the local authority, as well as by the buyer and seller themselves, are also dealt with here. An imaginary example is presented in detail. The letters that are written when Matthew Seaton deals with his own purchase of 14 Twintree Avenue, Minford, are set out verbatim, and the documents that are prepared are explained.

This book does not deal with new property, nor flats. It also does not deal with what happens when the house is in Scotland or Northern Ireland, where the procedure and the law are quite different.

This amended reprint has been brought up to date on substantive matters, but the price of the property and the dates of correspondence have not been altered.

People do not ask a solicitor to deal with the formalities involved in buying or selling a car or a washing machine. Why, and when, is it necessary to have a solicitor when buying a house?

A house cannot legally be transferred as easily as a car, or any other chattel. For instance, it is a legal requirement to have a deed (that is, a document which is not merely signed, but 'signed, sealed and delivered') in order that the buyer should become the owner of a house. Furthermore, there are enquiries of a legal nature that should be made about a house, to ensure that the buyer will be able to live in it as he intends. You pay a solicitor to take over the responsibility.

PROVING OWNERSHIP

The main function of the buyer's solicitor in the business of buying a house is to enquire into the ownership—or title, as lawyers call it—of the seller. This is done by examining a summary (called an abstract) of the title deeds covering the preceding 15 years or more. The abstract is prepared by the seller's solicitor. In this way the buyer's solicitor finds out whether the property was correctly transferred to previous owners, at any rate during that period. The amount of work involved depends on the circumstances: on how many times the property has changed hands, on the way in which the property was owned, on whether the various owners had mortgages, on whether other people had various rights over the property (rights of way, for instance) and on many other things. Every time the property changes hands, the solicitor for the buyer has to go through this rigmarole. He has to check how the previous transactions were carried out, even though, for instance, the house was last sold only the year before and the solicitor for the buyer went through the same procedure then. The buyer's solicitor is said to investigate the title; the seller's solicitor is said to deduce the title. Quite a lot of time can be involved in both of these processes.

LAND REGISTRATION

Towards the end of the last century, a new system to deal with the transfer of land was introduced. Land, by the way, includes any building on it; the owner may think mainly in terms of the bricks and mortar, but the lawyer is more inclined to think in terms of the land, including everything on it, such as buildings, and everything under it and over it. The essence of this new system of land transfer was that a government department should prepare a register of the ownership of land in England and Wales.

The Land Registration Acts now provide the legal basis for the system which is called land registration and the government department which operates it is called the Land Registry.

Every bit of land in England and Wales did not become registered land overnight. The staff at the Land Registry would have been overwhelmed, and there would have been chaos, especially where properties were currently changing hands. So the system of land registration is still being introduced gradually throughout the country. After a new area is added to the list of districts where registration is compulsory, the title to any property in that area has to be registered. This does not have to be done immediately, however, but only when the property is next sold. The buyer must then register the title. The result is that even though a particular property is in an area where registration is compulsory, the title to it may still be unregistered. This will be because it has not been sold since the date when registration became compulsory for that particular area.

To find out if registration is compulsory in any particular place, you can ask the Land Registry (Lincoln's Inn Fields, London WC2A 3PH, telephone 01-405 3488) for 'explanatory leaflet No. 9'. This sets out the counties and districts in England with the dates on which registration became compulsory there. It also lists the District Land Registries for each county.

The longer a particular area has had compulsory registration of title, the greater are the chances that a particular property in it already has a registered title. In Eastbourne, for example, where registration of title has been compulsory since 1926, there are comparatively few properties left where the title is not registered, for most properties will by now have been sold at least once since 1926. But in Bath, where registration only became compulsory in 1974, the majority of properties do not yet have registered titles—only those which have been sold since 1974, plus those few which were registered voluntarily. It used to be possible to register a title in a non-compulsory area, if the owner wanted to, but this is no longer so for a private owner.

Once the property is registered—or, to be more accurate, the title to the property is registered—the transfer of ownership becomes much more simple. Instead of having to wade through the deeds dealing with the ownership for the preceding 15 years or more, the buyer's solicitor has only to refer to the register kept at the Land Registry. If this shows that the seller is the owner, the buyer does not need to go to any further trouble on the question of ownership; the register of the property at the Land Registry is enough. If the title is registered, the deed transferring the property from the seller to the buyer, called a transfer, is quite short, and intelligible.

ENQUIRIES AND LOCAL SEARCHES

If the title is registered, therefore, the tasks of the solicitors in transferring ownership are often quite simple. However, certain things have to be done which are much the same whether the title is registered or unregistered.

There are many questions which the buyer's solicitor has to ask the seller's solicitor. This is done mainly on a printed form called 'enquiries before contract' and often spoken of as being 'preliminary enquiries'. This form asks questions about the boundaries of the property, about the way in which the main services (water, gas and electricity) are laid on, about rights of way, about planning consents and other planning matters, and about sanitary and other notices issued by the local authority, and many other things.

The buyer's solicitor also has to make what is called a local search. To do this, he sends a form to the local council (the district council or, in London, the borough council) and finds out whether any official claims are made against the property, for instance regarding money due for road charges. At the same time he sends another form to the local authority, asking a large number of questions about roads, public health, town and country planning, compulsory purchase and so on. By evaluating the results of his local search and enquiries, the solicitor makes sure, so far as can be done, that the local authority has not made any decisions which may affect the property, such as widening the road or designating the property to be of special architectural or historic interest.

MORTGAGE

Another important part of the solicitor's functions where a person is buying a house concerns the mortgage. The building society, or other lender, needs to be in a position where it can sell the property and repay itself out of the proceeds, if the buyer falls down on payments. It must be satisfied that the buyer will indeed be the owner when the present transaction is completed. So the building society's solicitor must investigate the title to the property, in much the same way as the buyer's solicitor does. Thus you get the seller's solicitor satisfying the buyer's solicitor about the title, followed by the buyer's solicitor satisfying the building society's solicitor about the title. In addition, the buyer's solicitor has to supply the building society's solicitor with all the other information he has obtained about the property. To do this, he sends to the building society's solicitor the local search and enquiries of the local authorities, with their replies, as well as the enquiries before contract with the replies. Finally, the buyer's solicitor has to approve the mortgage deed. He considers its legal effect, and if necessary tells the buyer what it all means. Where he deals also with a mortgage, the buyer's solicitor is entitled to be paid an additional fee on top of the fee he gets for dealing with the purchase. In practice, the same solicitor often acts for the buyer and for the building society—they are both clients of his in this particular transaction. There is unlikely to be any conflict of interest if a solicitor acts both for the buyer and for the building society. This saves a good deal of time and trouble, and saves the buyer money, too.

CONTRACT

The seller's solicitor starts the transaction by preparing the contract in draft, which he then sends (usually with a copy) to the buyer's solicitor for approval. The contract is the document by which, usually somewhere around half way through the transaction, the buyer and the seller formally commit themselves to go through with the deal. When signed and exchanged, it is a legally binding agreement to buy and to sell. The document which actually transfers the property comes later.

WORKING OUT THE MONEY

Part of the purchase price is often provided by the building society, which deducts from the loan certain costs, stamp duty, and other expenses. The rest of the money, after allowing for the deposit already paid, is provided by the buyer himself. Often the seller also has a mortgage which has to be paid off, in which case some of the purchase money goes to the seller and some to his building society. Finally, rates and water rates have to be apportioned between buyer and seller. The result is that working out the figures for completion can be quite difficult. It is up to the seller's solicitor to work out the apportionment of the rates and water rates, and any other outgoings (for instance, ground rent and insurance where the house is leasehold). He then tells the buyer's solicitor exactly how much money is needed to complete the sale, and how it is to be split—so much to the seller's building society, and the rest to the seller's solicitor, usually. The buyer's solicitor then works out where the money is coming from: so much from the building society the rest from the buyer himself.

OWNER OCCUPIER SELLING REGISTERED PROPERTY

Conveyancing in England and Wales is at its simplest when an owner occupier is selling a house with a registered title to a person who requires

owner occupier

the house for his own occupation. It is conveyancing in a case like this which this book describes, and no other. The matter gets more complicated where the title is not registered, since deducing and investigating an unregistered title is more complicated.

It is more complicated, too, where the house is newly built, particularly where it is part of a housing estate. In that case, the buyer's solicitor must first of all ensure that the contract provides that the house itself should be properly built. He has also to make sure that the boundaries of the property are correctly shown on the plans, that the seller is providing any rights of way, drainage and similar rights which may be necessary, and that the restrictions imposed by the seller are fair. Once these matters are settled for the first buyer, they are fixed more or less unalterably for the future, so that the solicitors acting for subsequent buyers are very much in the position of having to take things as they find them. It may well be that they would have dealt with them somewhat differently had they been acting for the buyer at that first purchase. There is often not much they can do when it comes to their turn. The solicitors for subsequent buyers are concerned only to understand the effect of the arrangements made when the house was sold for the first time and to tell their clients about them. The responsibilities on the legal side on the second and subsequent purchases are therefore considerably less than on that vital first purchase when the house was being built.

Other complications arise when part of the property is already let, and the buyer is taking over the sitting tenant. Where there is an existing tenancy, there may be difficulties which the buyer does not readily appreciate.

The procedure described in this book is inappropriate, too, for cases where a person takes a lease at a rent (not a ground rent) without paying a capital sum. This does not mean, however, that leasehold property is excluded from consideration here. It is, of course, quite common to find a house where the owner occupier is the holder of a lease which he has bought for a capital sum—where the property is a leasehold one, in fact, instead of a freehold. Special legal difficulties arise at the time when the lease is first granted, usually when the house is built, and such cases are excluded from consideration here. But once the lease is granted, and provided the title to it is registered (as it can be where the lease is granted for a term of at least 21 years), the procedure for the sale of a leasehold property is little different from the sale of a freehold, but the law is more complicated.

However, this book does not deal with the procedure by which the leaseholder acquires the freehold, something which has become more common since the Leasehold Reform Act 1967 gave him the right to buy the freehold in some cases.

Nor does this book deal with transfers of maisonettes or flats, that is to say transfers of a part or parts of a building where other parts of the building are used in common with other people. But that does not mean that terrace and semi-detached houses are excluded. Bungalows and cottages too, are included: they are covered by the word house.

Business premises are not dealt with here, as special legal problems may arise, even if part of the property is used to live in, as in the case of a flat over a shop.

Provided that the house is a second-hand one, at present fully occupied by an owner occupier, and the title to it is already registered, an intelligent and industrious non-lawyer should be able to buy or sell it without having a solicitor.

The buyer who contemplates taking through a transaction without a solicitor should ask the estate agent, or the seller himself: 'Is the whole house now occupied by the seller?' and 'Is the title registered?' The estate agent may not know the answer to the second question. Even the seller himself may not know. In the areas where registration of title is compulsory, particularly where it has been compulsory for some time, it is certainly worth asking whether the title is registered or not. In some counties, particularly those within striking distance of London, even though registration of title is not yet compulsory, it is quite possible that the title is registered already. But in parts of the country where registration is not yet compulsory it is rather unlikely that the title will be registered. If the title is not registered, the buyer should instruct his solicitor.

If the seller does not know whether his title is registered, he can find out from the title deeds. The property is registered if there is a large folder entitled 'Land Certificate' with the title deeds. Where there is a mortgage on the property, the folder is entitled 'Charge Certificate' and is held by the building society or other mortgagee.

SNAGS

Having taken a deep breath and decided that you will act for yourself when buying or selling a house, you must face the fact that it may turn out that you may not succeed in carrying it through. At each stage through the transaction something may turn up which will defeat you, and you will then—sheepishly, no doubt—have to take your file to a solicitor and get him to complete the matter for you. He will probably charge you the same as if he had carried it through from the beginning. He will probably not think highly of your efforts so far. He may say that he ought to charge you for unravelling the mess you have made of the matter on your own. All the same, do not delay going to a solicitor if you are in any doubt or difficulty.

Legal problems may arise in the course of a transaction. What, for instance, if the seller were to die or become bankrupt after a binding contract had been made, but before the transaction was completed? The do-it-yourself conveyancer must then go to a solicitor who should advise and act for him. There are a number of other situations where the layman may be forced into abandoning his efforts. For this reason, it is prudent to keep in reserve sufficient money to pay the solicitor's fees.

LEGALS FEES AND EXPENSES

Legal costs on the sale and purchase of a house depend on a number of things, including the price of the house. Solicitors used to charge fees on a scale laid down by law. Scale fees were abolished in 1973 and now they can charge whatever fee is fair and reasonable in the circumstances. Few solicitors are still using the old scale as a guide to what to charge now; most now charge considerably more than the old scale fees (and the difference in fees charged for conveyancing registered and unregistered property is getting smaller).

The buyer is generally involved in additional expenses, on top of his solicitor's fee. The total costs when buying are often considerably higher than the total costs when selling. These additional expenses thrown on to the buyer may include stamp duty, mortgage costs and Land Registry fees.

—STAMP DUTY

Stamp duty is payable to the government on certain documents, including deeds transferring houses or shares. The buyer pays no stamp duty on the transfer of a house where the price does not exceed £15000. Where the price is between £15001 and £20000, the stamp duty on the transfer is one half per cent, or, to be exact, it is 25p for every £50 and fraction of £50 of the price. Thus, where the price is £18000, the stamp duty on the transfer amounts to £90. Where the price is between £20001 and £25000, the duty is one per cent; between £25001 and £30000 the duty is 1½ per cent; over £30000 it is 2 per cent—again, to be exact, it is £1 for every £50 of the price. On a purchase at £32000, therefore, stamp duty is £640.

—MORTGAGE COSTS

If the buyer has a mortgage, there are additional solicitors' fees to be paid. Where the mortgage is with a building society, the building society's solicitor has to be paid a fee for dealing with the building society's side of the mortgage. There is a recommended scale of solicitors' fees for the legal work involved in dealing with mortgages up to £25000.

In addition, the buyer's own solicitor is also entitled to charge an extra fee for dealing with his, the borrower's side of the mortgage: this includes satisfying the building society's solicitor about the title, and approving the mortgage deed. The buyer has to pay both fees, as normally a loan from a building society is made on condition that the buyer reimburses the building society for its legal costs and the other expenses.

Local authorities also adopt the building society scale. Other lenders such as insurance companies often do so, too, although they do not have to. Where the lender is not a building society or a local authority, the buyer might find that the solicitors' fees, both those of his own solicitor and of the lender's, are higher.

—LAND REGISTRY FEES

Where the title to a property is already registered, the buyer has to register at the Land Registry the transfer of ownership to him, and is charged a fee for doing this. The Land Registry fees are on a scale, so the amount payable depends on the price paid. Also, the building society will require that its interest in the property, by virtue of the mortgage, should be entered on the register. There is no fee for registering the mortgage if it is granted at the time of purchase, as normally happens, and the registration of both is made simultaneously. If, as occasionally happens, the mortgage is made at some time after the house was bought, a scale fee based on the amount of the mortgage is charged for registration.

—SAVING IN FEES

The man who sells his house without having a solicitor saves himself the fee paid to solicitors. When selling, there are few, if any, other expenses involved. Where a mortgage is paid off at the time of the sale, there may be a fee to be paid to the building society's solicitor (around £10).

The man who buys his house without having a solicitor likewise saves himself the fee paid to solicitors. Where he has a mortgage, his solicitor's fee for dealing with the mortgage is also saved. But that is all. All other expenses involved, including stamp duty, Land Registry fees, and the building society's solicitor's fee, still have to be paid. So when buying a house with a registered title for £16000, with a mortgage of £13000, he could be saving upwards of £150 on solicitors' fees.

THE REGISTER

The transfer of a property with a registered title is made by reference to its register at the Land Registry. When there is no mortgage, the owner has a land certificate containing a copy of the entries on the register. So long as the property is mortgaged, however, the land certificate is kept at the Land Registry, and instead there is a charge certificate issued to the building society, or whoever else is the lender. The charge certificate is almost the same as a land certificate, and contains a copy of the entries on the register; these include particulars of the mortgage. Whether there is a mortgage or not, the owner and anyone who has his written permission can obtain a photocopy of the entries on the register, by applying to the Land Registry and paying a small fee.

Each registered property has its own title number, and it is impossible to deal with registered land without reference to its title number. The register is headed with the title number.

The register of every property is divided into three parts: the property register, the proprietorship register, and the charges register.

THE PROPERTY REGISTER

The property register contains a description of the property. The county and district are separately stated, followed by a description of the property itself. In the case of a freehold house in a built-up area, for instance in the suburb of a city, it is likely to be quite a straightforward description such as: 'The Freehold land shown and edged with red on the plan of the above Title filed at the Registry registered on 8 January 1948 being land and buildings on the north side of Acacia Avenue . . .', followed by a later entry, made after the house was first occupied, saying: 'Property now known as 26 Acacia Avenue'. The entry might just read: '26 Acacia

Avenue' with a reference to the Land Registry General Map (for example Parcel No. 158, London Sheet VI.68, Section B) or to a filed plan.

Where the property is leasehold, the property register contains a description of the lease: its date, who granted it, to whom, the date from when the lease runs, for how many years, the amount of the ground rent, and the price paid for the lease, as well as a description of the property as contained in the lease. The register itself does not set out the lease in full. Where the property is leasehold, the lease is, if anything, more important than the register.

In the case of both freehold and leasehold property, the property register refers to a plan. This plan is at the heart of registered conveyancing. A copy of the plan is bound into the land certificate (or charge certificate, if there is a mortgage). It shows part of the locality with the property itself usually coloured or outlined in red. The description of the property given in the property register and the plan together give a reliable identification of the boundaries of the property.

The property register sometimes includes a description of certain rights which go with the house. For instance, a property may have a right of way, or some similar right over another property. Such a right really forms part of the property itself, as it may constitute a valuable asset which enables the occupier to live in, or use the house, more effectively. It is logical, therefore, that the property register should contain a description of this sort of right. Sometimes such rights are set out with an elaborate description, and excerpts from the deed or deeds which created them may be quoted. These are unlikely to be written in language that a layman will readily understand, but it is seldom difficult to gather the gist of what they are all about.

THE PROPRIETORSHIP REGISTER

This contains the name and address of the person registered as being the owner, that is, the registered proprietor. In addition, under the heading 'Proprietorship Register' should appear the words 'Title Absolute'. This implies that the person whose name is entered in the register is guaranteed to be the owner, and his title to the property cannot be challenged. This is the main point of having a registered title; the person who first registered that property had to satisfy the Land Registry that he really was the owner, and that there were no snags that could arise. Having done so, he became registered as the owner with title absolute. It is possible for an applicant to fail to satisfy the requirements of the Land Registry about title. If this happens, the registry may allow the applicant to register his title, but not with title absolute; he will instead be given what is called a possessory title. If, in the heading to the proprietorship register, the words 'Possessory Title' or 'Qualified Title' appear, instead of the words 'Title Absolute', the position of the buyer is not much better than that of the person buying a house which does not have a registered title at all.

In the case of leasehold property, the heading to the proprietorship register may state that the owner is registered either with title absolute or with good leasehold title. In practice, good leasehold, unlike possessory title, is acceptable.

Whether the title is leasehold or freehold, the proprietorship register may contain a statement of the price paid for the property by the owner. Because of this, it is unusual for the seller to let the buyer see a copy of the proprietorship register, containing the price, until after exchange of contracts—until the buyer has legally committed himself to a price. Otherwise, the buyer might be influenced in deciding what price he should pay. Entries regarding property that has been sold since 1976 may now not include the price.

It is usual for the Land Registry to add the new owner's name to the proprietorship register when a property changes hands, and just strike through the name of the seller. Thus, you often find that the proprietorship register consists of a list of names and addresses and prices paid, all but the last of which have been struck through. The name that is left in the proprietorship register is the name of the present registered proprietor.

THE CHARGES REGISTER

This part of the register contains details of rights which other people have over, or in respect of, the property. They are rights and interests which detract from, or take something away from, the owner's property as described in the property register, and they are sometimes referred to as incumbrances. Two kinds are most commonly found: restrictive covenants and mortgages.

Restrictive covenants have long been a feature of conveyancing. When a landowner sells off a large piece of land which is to be turned into a housing estate, he usually requires the builder (or other developer) to undertake that certain conditions shall in future be complied with. He may insist, for example, that not more than so many houses to the acre should be built on the land. Likewise, the builder, when he comes to sell off the new house to the first owners, may require each of them to undertake that the houses should not, for instance, be turned into a shop, nor that any new building—a garage, or garden shed, perhaps—should be put nearer than so many feet to the road. In both cases, these restrictions are made in the form of written covenants set out in the deed that transfers the property from the seller to the buyer. The buyer is said to enter into restrictive covenants with the seller, and the object is usually to do this in such a way that not only the first buyer, but all subsequent owners also, should be bound by the covenants. Normally, they are quite reasonable and unlikely to prevent a buyer from doing anything he wants to do with the property. They can be of advantage to individual house owners, because they generally operate throughout the neighbourhood. Sometimes one finds an unrealistic covenant: for instance 'Washing shall not be hung out to dry'.

There are complicated rules about how far restrictive covenants can be enforced after the property has changed hands. Just because a covenant appears in the charges register at the Land Registry it does not mean necessarily that the covenant can currently be enforced against the present owner. Many cannot. But the person buying a house should assume that all covenants set out in the charges register can in fact be enforced against him when he becomes the owner. If they forbid the doing of anything which in any way affects what he proposes to do with the property, he should either take legal advice on the point, or look for another house. He will normally be sent a copy of the restrictive covenants right at the beginning of the transaction when the seller's solicitor sends him the draft contract. The contract may describe them as being 'covenants, conditions and stipulations', or something like that.

The charges register deals with restrictive covenants by setting out a list of the deeds which contained them. For example, an entry in the charges register might read as follows:

15 April 1955—A conveyance dated 2 October 1924 made between (1) William George Nolan (Vendor) and (2) John Henry Davidson (Purchaser) contains covenants, particulars of which are set out in the Schedule of Restrictive Covenants annexed hereto.

At the end of the charges register would appear the schedule, where the covenants themselves are set out in full. But if the covenants are short, they may be set out in the charges register itself, without having a separate schedule.

The charges register also contains particulars of any mortgages. There is an entry—in two parts—in the charges register dealing with each mortgage. It looks something like this:

2 14 November 1962—CHARGE dated 7 November 1962 registered on 14 November 1962 to secure the moneys therein mentioned.

3 PROPRIETOR—ABBEY NATIONAL BUILDING SOCIETY of Abbey House, Baker Street, N.W.1, registered on 14 November 1962.

The mortgage is described in the register as a charge and this, indeed, it is. The building society that lent the money is described as being the proprietor of the charge. In the proprietorship register, on the other hand, the name that appears is that of the owner of the property. A person is still the legal owner, even if there is a mortgage on the house.

One reason why particulars of an existing mortgage are included in the charges register is to protect the building society, or whoever it was who lent the money which is secured by the mortgage. Unless these particulars were there, a fraudulent owner might induce an innocent buyer to part with the purchase price on the assurance that there was no mortgage. If this were to happen, and the fraudulent seller were to disappear without paying off the mortgage, there would be a contest between the buyer and the building society about who was entitled to what. So the building society protects its position by having entries, such as those above, made in the charges register, and the buyer, on looking at the register, as he does when he is in the process of buying the house, cannot fail to see them. But the buyer can and should insist that the mortgage be completely paid off before he becomes the owner. The seller's building society, on the other hand, is not going to allow the entries in the charges register, which give it protection, to be removed until the mortgage money has been paid in full. This cannot be done until the sale is completed and the buyer hands over the price. Here, then, is something of an impasse.

It is resolved in this way. When the buyer sees that the seller still has a mortgage, he will tell the seller's solicitor (although it is obvious) that he will require that the existing mortgage should be paid off at completion. When it comes to completing the transaction, all the necessary documents to confer ownership on the buyer are handed over in exchange for the money. The building society's solicitor takes what is due to pay off the mortgage and in exchange hands over the charge certificate which contains the mortgage deed. In addition, the building society has to signify that its claim against the property has ceased. The building society hands over a separate document, called form 53, which acknowledges that the mortgage is at an end.

The buyer can then apply to the Land Registry who will, on the strength of form 53, cross out the entries in the charges register relating to the seller's mortgage. In their place, particulars of the buyer's mortgage—if any—will be entered.

SEARCHING THE REGISTER

The whole of the register relating to a property—property register, proprietorship register and charges register—is private; it is not open to public inspection. All that anybody can find out is whether or not a particular property is registered, and if so, what its title number is. He would not be able to find out who is the owner, nor the price paid for it, nor any other information shown on the register, without the written permission of the registered owner.

In practice, there is only one situation in which it is commonly necessary for someone else to have access to the register. Immediately after the buyer and seller have entered into a binding contract to buy and sell, the seller sends to the buyer a copy of the entries on the register. This is usually a photocopy, showing also the date on which it was issued by the Land Registry. But the crucial date, so far as the buyer is concerned, is a little later on. It is the completion date, when he finally hands over his money and accepts the transfer of the property from the seller. How can the buyer be sure that, between the date on which the Land Registry issued the photocopy of the entries on the register and the completion date, there has not been some change on the register? For all he knows in the meantime someone else may have become registered as the owner, or some new mortgage may have been made. The buyer makes certain that there has been no change in the state of the register between the date stamped on the photocopy and the date of completion, by making a search. To make the search, he needs to have the written permission of the seller, that is, an authority from the registered proprietor to inspect the register.

Thus, a few days before completion, the buyer's solicitor sends off to the Land Registry a search form, known as form 94A, and also an authority from the owner to inspect the register, as the registry will not answer a form 94A without such an authority. The Land Registry will straightaway send back a search certificate, stating whether there has been any change in the register since the day on which the photocopy of the entries on the register was issued. If there is no change, the buyer knows he can safely complete his purchase.

Sometimes, the seller's solicitor does not send an official photocopy of the entries on the register. Instead, he makes his own copy of the land certificate; his own photocopy, perhaps, or even just a typed copy. What does the buyer do then? In this case the buyer safeguards his position by finding out in advance from the seller's solicitor when the land certificate was last brought up to date by the Land Registry. Every time there is a transaction, the land certificate should be sent to the Land Registry, so that the appropriate alterations can be made. The idea is that it should at all times contain a true copy of the register itself, the one kept at the registry. But it is just possible that some change could have taken place— a compulsory mortgage under a High Court order, for instance—without the land certificate having been sent to the registry to be brought up to date. Perhaps the owner refused to send it. The buyer wants to be sure that the land certificate is in fact up to date, and this he does by making a search. The land certificate has stamped in it the date when it was last compared with the actual register in the Land Registry. Therefore the search—on form 94A, once again—merely asks whether there have been any changes in the register since that date. If the Land Registry's reply— again it comes in the form of a search certificate—shows that there have been no such changes, the buyer knows that he is safe. Accordingly, when the seller (or his solicitor) sends a typed copy of the land certificate, he has to state the date when the land certificate was last compared with the register. There is no doubt that it is much easier all round if the seller obtains for the buyer's use a photocopy from the Land Registry, rather than make his own copy.

The final few days between the date on which the registry issues a search certificate and the date on which the buyer lodges in the registry his application to be registered as the new owner are covered by a special rule. This rule gives the buyer, who made the search, priority for 20 working days over anybody else, so that there is virtually no possibility of the buyer parting with his money without getting ownership. If anybody else makes a search in the relevant 20 days, the earlier search will be shown as a claim to priority over the second search, and revealed as such on the second search certificate. The "second buyer" or lender is therefore warned off, and should not complete his deal.

do-it-yourself conveyancer

The main stages of the legal side of buying a house

STAGE	SENT BY	SENT TO
1. Application for mortgage	buyer	building society
2. Instruction to surveyor	buyer	his surveyor
3. Draft contract	seller	buyer
4. Enquiries before contract (form: Conveyancing 29 Long)	buyer	seller
5. Local search (forms: LLC1 and Con. 29 London or England and Wales)	buyer	local authority
6. Answers to enquiries before contract	seller	buyer
7. Approval of draft contract	buyer	seller
8. Mortgage offer	building society	buyer
9. Surveyor's report	surveyor	buyer
10. Local search certificate	local authority	buyer
11. }Exchange of	buyer	seller
12. }contracts	seller	buyer
13. Copy of entries on register and authority to inspect register	seller	buyer
14. Requisitions on title (form: Con. 28B)	buyer	seller
15. Draft transfer (form: 19)	buyer	seller
16. Answers to requisitions on title	seller	buyer
17. Approval of transfer	seller	buyer
18. Copy of entries, plan, contract, enquiries before contract, requisitions on title, local authority search, draft transfer	buyer	building society
19. Requisitions on title	building society	buyer
20. Answers to requisitions on title	buyer	building society
21. Draft mortgage deed	building society	buyer
22. Completion statement	seller	buyer
23. Mortgage deed	building society	buyer
24. Land Registry search	buyer	Land Registry
25. Search certificate (form: 94A)	Land Registry	buyer
26. Completion		
27. *Transfer to be stamped within one month	buyer	stamp office or main post office
28. *Transfer to be registered	buyer	Land Registry

* if no mortgage

CONVEYANCING

Buyer

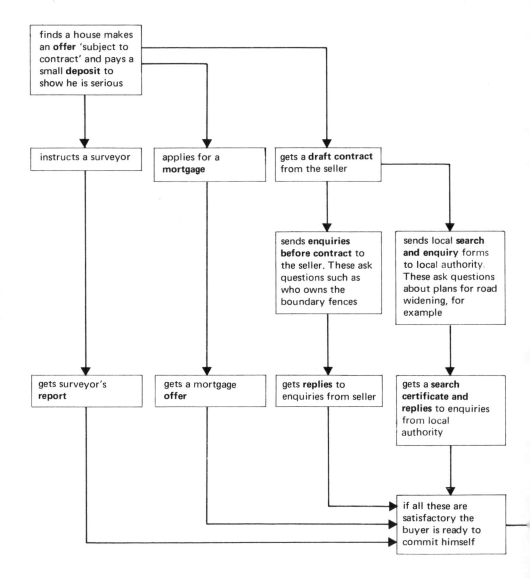

finds a house makes an **offer** 'subject to contract' and pays a small **deposit** to show he is serious

instructs a surveyor

applies for a **mortgage**

gets a **draft contract** from the seller

sends **enquiries before contract** to the seller. These ask questions such as who owns the boundary fences

sends local **search and enquiry** forms to local authority. These ask questions about plans for road widening, for example

gets surveyor's **report**

gets a mortgage **offer**

gets **replies** to enquiries from seller

gets a **search certificate and replies** to enquiries from local authority

if all these are satisfactory the buyer is ready to commit himself

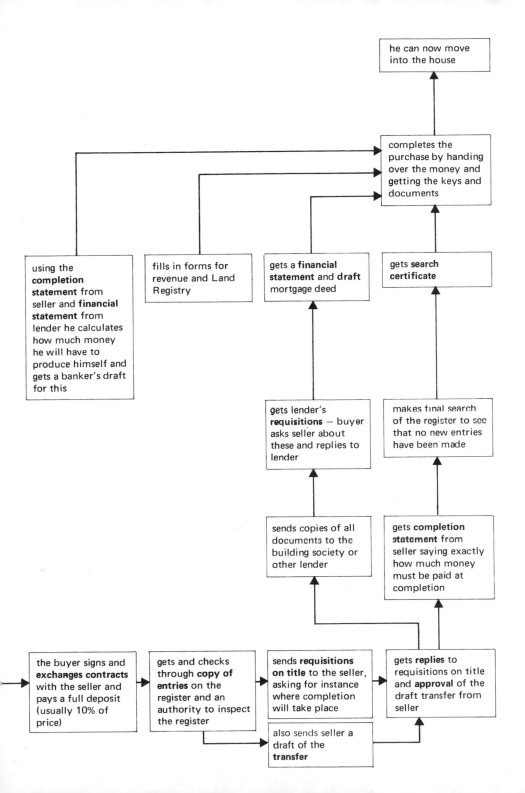

he can now move into the house

completes the purchase by handing over the money and getting the keys and documents

using the **completion statement** from seller and **financial statement** from lender he calculates how much money he will have to produce himself and gets a banker's draft for this

fills in forms for revenue and Land Registry

gets a **financial statement** and **draft** mortgage deed

gets **search certificate**

gets lender's **requisitions** – buyer asks seller about these and replies to lender

makes final search of the register to see that no new entries have been made

sends copies of all documents to the building society or other lender

gets **completion statement** from seller saying exactly how much money must be paid at completion

the buyer signs and **exchanges contracts** with the seller and pays a full deposit (usually 10% of price)

gets and checks through **copy of entries** on the register and an authority to inspect the register

sends **requisitions on title** to the seller, asking for instance where completion will take place

gets **replies** to requisitions on title and **approval** of the draft transfer from seller

also sends seller a draft of the **transfer**

The main participants

THE BUYER
Matthew J. Seaton,
38 Broadstone Drive,
Hastings, Sussex.

THE SELLER
William H. Timms,
14 Twintree Avenue,
Minford, Surrey.

THE SELLER'S SOLICITORS
Dodds & Son,
1 Charter Street,
Minford, Surrey.

THE BUYER'S BUILDING SOCIETY
Forthright Building Society,
88 Lomax Street,
Minford, Surrey.

THE SELLER'S BUILDING SOCIETY
Minford Building Society,
102 Great Winchester Street,
Minford, Surrey.

THE BUYER'S BUILDING SOCIETY'S
   SOLICITORS
Hodgson, Green & Co.,
67 Lomax Street,
Minford, Surrey.

THE SELLER'S BUILDING SOCIETY'S
   SOLICITORS
Anderson, James & Pringle,
88 Great Winchester Street,
Minford, Surrey.

THE BUYER'S INSURANCE COMPANY
Bridstow Insurance Co. Ltd.,
403 High Street,
Guildford, Surrey.

THE SELLER'S AGENTS
Flint & Morgan,
43 High Street,
Minford, Surrey.

THE BUYER'S SURVEYORS
Andrew Robertson & Co.,
22 Hamilton Street,
Minford, Surrey.

ESTATE AGENTS

The story of Matthew Seaton, a young school teacher, begins when the house was found. Flint & Morgan, the estate agents, had sent him particulars of 14 Twintree Avenue, Minford, Surrey, in the same way as they, and other agents, had sent many before. The limit the Seatons had set themselves was £16000; the price asked for 14 Twintree Avenue was £17500. Acting quickly, they had, on the day the details were received from Flint & Morgan, gone straight to Minford to see the house. They liked it. But the price was higher than their limit.

At Flint & Morgan's office in Minford High Street, Matthew had assumed an air of casual interest. 'We like it,' he said, 'but it's not worth £17500 to us. We would pay £16000 for it, but that's our limit' as indeed it was. 'You don't get much for that round here, you know' said Mr Morgan, 'I advised the owners what price they should ask for the place, of course, and I think they could get it, but I'll see what they say to your offer. I must put to my clients any offer I receive, you know.'

Mr Morgan left the room, no doubt to speak more candidly on the telephone to his client, Mr Timms. The Seatons said nothing in his absence, but each knew that what was now being discussed would affect their future. Mr Morgan came back. 'They will take £16250 for a quick sale' he said. Matthew looked at his wife; he sensed assent. 'All right, we'll have it' he said. This was it.

Matthew sensed assent

Matthew was prepared for what was now to follow. He had realised that he would be needing a mortgage when the time came. He had already spoken to someone at the Forthright Building Society, with whom he had had dealings before, and hoped there would be no undue difficulty in getting the mortgage he wanted. There were already several people interested in buying his present house, and he could now seek a firm offer for it. He knew that he would not be able to sign a binding contract to buy 14 Twintree Avenue until a buyer had signed a binding contract to buy his present house.

Mr Morgan asked Matthew whether he needed help in getting a mortgage. Even if he had not already approached the Forthright Building Society, Matthew would not necessarily have taken up Mr Morgan's offer, but would have made his own choice of building society. An estate agent may well be concerned to promote one particular building society, irrespective of whether it is likely to be the best one for the buyer's particular circumstances.

Mr Morgan raised the question of a deposit. Matthew had noticed that Mr Morgan had the letters MNAEA after his name, on the firm's headed notepaper. This meant that he was a member of the National Association of Estate Agents, one of the professional bodies which operate a scheme to protect deposits paid by purchasers. If an estate agent has no letters after his name and does not belong to an organisation which provides such an insurance scheme, a buyer should be wary of paying him a deposit. If there is no estate agent, the buyer can pay a preliminary deposit to the seller's solicitor, or, if he has no solicitor, he should open a joint account with the seller.

Matthew agreed to leave a cheque for £100, just to show he was serious in wishing to buy the house. 'Of course, this is subject to contract at this stage' he told Mr Morgan. 'And subject to survey' he cautiously added. He might wish to revise his offer, should his survey prove unfavourable.

It was arranged that Flint & Morgan would send by post a receipt for the £100 paid towards the deposit. If Matthew had paid this £100 in cash, he would have insisted on having a receipt there and then. 'Who are the solicitors who will be acting for you on the legal side?' asked Mr Morgan. 'I shall be doing my own conveyancing' said Matthew.

'Is the title registered, do you know?' asked Matthew. 'I assume so, but I will check if you like. I think it must be, as Mr Timms has only been there about ten years, I believe' said Mr Morgan. 'I'd be grateful if you would make sure and let me know' said Matthew. Yes, he thought, if the seller has been there since about 1964, the title must be registered, as registration of title has been compulsory in Surrey since 1952.

'I take it that the owner is living in the house and that there aren't any tenants or anything like that' said Matthew. 'Yes, Mr Timms is living there, with the family, and as far as I know there are no lodgers' said Mr Morgan. 'One final point, what is the local authority?' 'Minford District Council.'

a house of architectural distinction

MORTGAGE APPLICATION

Most house buyers need to borrow at least part of the price of a house; they need a mortgage, in fact. Matthew was no exception. It is not usually necessary to have a solicitor help in applying for a mortgage. A solicitor can, however, be useful in advising a buyer where to go for a mortgage, particularly if there is some feature of the circumstances, such as an aged house or buyer, or a house of architectural distinction, which may make it difficult to raise a loan in the ordinary way. Matthew planned to get his loan from the building society in which he had some money invested and with which he had had previous dealings. Other possible sources would have been an insurance company, the local authority, his bank or private trustees.

Current economic conditions in the country very much determine the ease with which a loan may be obtained. In recent years, there have been times when it has been very difficult to get a mortgage anywhere. At other times, the house buyer has had more choice.

So far as interest rates are concerned, there is often not much to choose between the various building societies. Many societies belong to the Building Societies Association, the members of which usually all charge the same rate of interest at any one time. There may, however, be differences between different building societies on the question of legal costs. Many building societies adopt a system whereby a large number of solicitors up and down the country are all authorised to act as solicitors to the building society. Where this happens there is a good chance that the same solicitor will be able to act for the building society and for the buyer.

The general rule is that the buyer pays the society's legal fees, whether or not the same solicitor is acting for both. Some societies used to pay their own legal costs in connection with a mortgage; this too, of course, saved the buyer some money, a considerable sum if the mortgage was for several thousand pounds. Where the same solicitor acts for the buyer and the building society, the recommended scale fee for his work for the building society is lower than the fee for the same work acting for the building society only.

Local authorities often provide mortgages, particularly for cheaper and older properties. There was a time when the rate of interest under a local authority mortgage, once fixed at the start, never varied throughout the life of the mortgage. But now they are like building society mortgages, and are liable to be raised and—occasionally—lowered, according to economic trends.

Some insurance companies lend money to enable people to buy houses. But it is necessary to take out an insurance policy with the company at the same time. This is called an endowment assurance policy, under which a capital sum becomes payable by the insurance company after premiums have been paid for a specific period, say 20 years, or on earlier death. There are many different variations on this form of life assurance.

The basis of a repayment mortgage is that the whole of the sum borrowed is to be repaid over a period of years by equal monthly instalments. Where this operates, each payment represents a bit of interest and a bit of capital. In the early years each payment will be nearly all interest and in the later years nearly all capital. This is important from the point of view of tax relief, as only interest is allowed against tax. Tax relief on mortgage interest is of benefit only to people paying income tax. People who pay low income tax, or none at all, can opt for paying a rate of interest somewhat below the usual rate and in return forgo tax relief on the interest. Once you have decided to have an option mortgage (as it is called) rather than tax relief, you cannot afterwards change your mind for four years.

It is sometimes possible to get a loan to buy a house and pay interest on the loan only, leaving the whole loan outstanding. Such a mortgage is usually combined with an endowment assurance policy, providing life assurance as well, and is called an endowment mortgage. This type of mortgage can be with a building society or with an insurance company. When the endowment policy, which is for the same amount as the sum borrowed on mortgage, reaches maturity, the capital sum then due is used to pay off the mortgage loan.

Other differences between a repayment and an endowment mortgage are that an endowment type costs more per month, particularly if it is a with-profits one. If the mortgage interest goes up, the length of payment time of a repayment mortgage can usually be extended; with an endowment mortgage, however, the monthly interest payments increase. Also, the insurance premiums, which eventually produce the capital sum to pay off the loan, are eligible for tax relief at about half the basic rate of tax, and all the interest is allowed against tax at the highest rate you pay. (With a repayment mortgage, only the payment of interest, not paying off the loan, is allowed against tax.) If the borrower of an endowment mortgage dies before the mortgage is paid off, his family does not have the financial burden of the repayments: the endowment assurance policy pays all that is due.

Banks lend money on mortgage too, but usually on more expensive property. The rates of interest are not fixed, so the borrower may have to increase his mortgage payments when the base rate changes. Sometimes a buyer is unable to sell the old house before the purchase of the new one is completed and a temporary bank loan is then used to bridge the gap. Matthew did not know at this stage whether he would be needing a bridging loan eventually.

Trustees and other organisations, as well as some private individuals, sometimes lend money on mortgage for house purchase. Trustees, unlike building societies, are often restricted to lending not more than two-thirds of the value of a property. Some solicitors are a good source of mortgages of this kind. If a solicitor finds you a mortgage, he is entitled to charge you a negotiating fee for doing so, on top of his fees for doing the legal work on the mortgage. The negotiating fee is not on a fixed scale and the solicitor can charge whatever is fair and reasonable. There are also brokers through whom it is possible to find mortgages.

From whatever source a loan is sought, it may take a little time to make the arrangements. There is likely to be a certain amount of form filling, and most lenders check references in order to satisfy themselves about the buyer's financial position and prospects. The sooner the buyer applies for his mortgage the better.

Matthew Seaton, therefore, went straight from the estate agent's office to the local office of the Forthright Building Society. He told the manager that his quest for a house was at an end, he hoped, and that he would like to apply for a loan from the society of £13000 which was 80 per cent of the price. He knew that he was unlikely to get more without providing additional security, perhaps in the form of a special type of life assurance policy.

It is easy to underestimate the expenses involved in buying a house. Matthew had already made a rough estimate that he should be able to manage, provided that the building society would lend him the £13000.

The manager gave him a formidable application form; one part of the form asked for information about himself and the other for information about the house.

Two days later he received the first letter to go on his file:

Flint & Morgan   *43, High Street,*
Surveys   *Minford, Surrey.*
Estate Agents   *20th May, 1974.*

Dear Sir,
re: 14 Twintree Avenue, Minford
We confirm your call at this office today, when you agreed to proceed with the purchase of the above property from our client, W. H. Timms, Esq, at the price of £16250, subject to contract. We confirm that you have paid a preliminary deposit of £100 for which we enclose our receipt.
We understand that you intend to deal with the legal formalities yourself. Messrs. Dodds & Son of this town will be acting as solicitors for Mr Timms.
We confirm that the title to the property is registered.
        Yours faithfully,
        Flint & Morgan
M. J. Seaton, Esq.

The receipt was enclosed:

Flint & Morgan   *43, High Street,*
Surveyors   *Minford, Surrey.*
Estate Agents   *20th May, 1974.*
re: 14 Twintree Avenue, Minford
RECEIVED of M. J. Seaton, Esq, of 38, Broadstone Drive, Hastings, Sussex, the sum of One Hundred Pounds [£100] as a preliminary deposit in respect of his purchase of the above freehold property from W. H. Timms, Esq, at the price of £16250; subject to contract, subject to survey.
        With thanks
        Flint & Morgan

GETTING THE FORMS

Oyez Publishing Ltd (a subsidiary of the Solicitors' Law Stationery Society Ltd) publishes legal books and documents. There are shops in Birmingham, Bristol, Cardiff, Manchester, Sheffield, Leeds and Liverpool, as well as London, where the necessary forms can be bought. Matthew telephoned Oyez House (01-407 8055) to find out how much a set of forms would cost in order to carry the whole purchase through. He then sent the following letter:

38 Broadstone Drive,
Hastings, Sussex.
21 May 1974.

Dear Sirs,
Please supply me with the necessary forms for doing my own house conveyancing. I enclose a cheque for £3.80 to cover postage, packing, VAT and handling charge.
Yours faithfully,
M. J. Seaton

Oyez Stationery Ltd,
Oyez House,
237 Long Lane,
London SE1 4PU.

These were the forms he received:

3 prints of Enquiries before contract (Conveyancing 29 Long)

3 prints of Requisitions on title (Con. 28B)

3 prints of Enquiries of district councils (Con. 29A England and Wales)

2 prints of Register of local land charges Requisition for search and official certificate of search (LLCI)

6 prints of Transfer of whole (19)

2 prints of Application by purchaser for Official Search with priority in respect of the Whole of the land in a title (94A)

2 prints of Application to register dealings with the Whole of the land comprised in registered titles (A4)

2 prints of Application for office copies (A44)

2 prints of Application for an official search of the index map (96)

2 prints of Application for an official search not applicable to registered land (K15)

2 prints of Application for an official search (Bankruptcy only) (K16)

If the house had been in London, Matthew would have had to ask for copies of Enquiries of local authority (form Con 29D London) instead of form Con 29A England and Wales. For property being bought by joint buyers, ask for form 19 JP instead of form 19. Matthew had already found out that the property was registered, so he did not really need forms 96 or K15, but they came anyway. He could have bought all but the first three forms on the list from Her Majesty's Stationery Office.

Another form he would be needing later was a land valuation form L(A) 451, available from a head post office or Inland Revenue Stamp Office.

THE MORTGAGE

Matthew now completed the application for a mortgage from the Forthright Building Society, and wrote:

> *38 Broadstone Drive,*
> *Hastings, Sussex.*
> *21 May 1974.*

Dear Sir,

> *14 Twintree Avenue, Minford*

As arranged at our discussion yesterday, I now enclose an application for a mortgage loan. The purchase price is £16250, and I would like to borrow £13000 from you, as shown on the form.

I also enclose my cheque for the surveyor's fee regarding valuation for the purposes of my proposed mortgage.

I intend to instruct the firm of surveyors who are preparing the valuation for your society to carry out a structural survey for me, at the same time; I shall therefore be glad if you will put me in touch with them.

> *Yours faithfully,*
> *M. J. Seaton*

The Manager,
Forthright Building Society.

If a house is to be bought in the joint names of husband and wife, this should be made clear in the mortgage application: both must sign the form.

VALUATION AND SURVEY

A building society always requires a surveyor's report before lending money on the mortgage of a house, and other lenders, local authorities, insurance companies, banks and trustees require one, too. The property is the security for their money, so they have to be satisfied about its value. The buyer generally has to pay the surveyor's fee, even though the building society, or whoever it is, will not let him see the surveyor's report. Members of the Building Societies Association operate a fixed scale for surveyors' fees, and the amount the buyer has to pay depends on the price being paid for the house, not on the amount of the loan sought or granted.

If the price of property is:	*Cost of valuation + VAT*
less than £15000	£5 + £1 for each £500 (or part thereof) by which price exceeds £2000
£15000 to £30000	£31 + £1 for each £1000 (or part thereof) by which price exceeds £15000
£30000 to £40000	£46 + £1 for each £2000 (or part thereof) by which price exceeds £30000
£40000 +	no set scale

Thus, on a price of £16250, the building society valuation fee worked out at £33, plus VAT.

Matthew received an acknowledgment to his mortgage application.

Forthright Building Society   *88 Lomax Street,*
Minford, Surrey.
23rd May, 1974.

Dear Sir,

                        14 Twintree Avenue, Minford

Thank you for your letter of 21st May enclosing application for an advance. I shall let you know the result of your application in due course. The Society's surveyor is arranging to inspect and report as soon as possible. I enclose a receipt in respect of the surveyor's fee.

In reply to your question, the firm of surveyors who will prepare the valuation are Messrs Andrew Robertson & Co, 22 Hamilton Street, Minford. I have spoken to Mr James Robertson on the telephone and he will be glad to carry out a survey of the house for you at the time of doing our valuation. He is expecting instructions from you on this matter.

                        Yours faithfully,
                        M. C. Templeton
                        Manager

M. J. Seaton, Esq.

Matthew therefore phoned Andrew Robertson & Co., the firm of chartered surveyors to arrange for an independent survey of the house for his own benefit, on top of the one the Forthright Building Society would be having from the firm. Some buyers tend to place some reliance on the fact that the survey on the house carried out for the building society must be satisfactory, otherwise the building society would not authorise the mortgage. This is not necessarily so. The surveyor is then acting for the building society, and not for the buyer, even though the buyer pays his fee. Even if he were to fail in his duty and the buyer was involved in great expense, the buyer would have no claim against him at all. Furthermore, all that the building society wants to know from the surveyor is the value of the property. Of course, the condition of the property, structurally and otherwise, affects its value. But the buyer can by no means conclude that, because the property has a certain value, there is nothing wrong with it which is not apparent.

If the buyer wants to know the condition of the property, he has to have another survey carried out on his own behalf, and has, of course, to pay for it. But there is no reason why he should not employ the same firm of surveyors as are preparing the valuation for the building society. The chances are that there will be an overall saving in fees by doing this, as there need only be one visit by one professional surveyor to the house. However, if the surveyor is on the staff of the building society, he may not be able to carry out a private structural survey for the buyer at the same time.

The cost of the independent survey should be agreed in advance. It depends on the size of the house and the time spent there and how thorough a survey is required. Sometimes the house is still furnished at the time when the surveyor is to make his examination so he will not be able to make as detailed a survey as if the house were empty. The surveyor may advise against buying the house unless he is given a chance to make a thorough examination, including lifting the carpets, for instance.

It is not only with old property that it is desirable to have a survey. Comparatively newly built houses can have serious defects, through bad design, bad materials, bad workmanship or neglect, or a combination of them. For a small fee, or even without an extra fee, a surveyor will sometimes advise the buyer on the value of the house. But a scale fee is payable by the buyer if he himself asks for a formal valuation.

Matthew had agreed a fee of £79.50 (VAT included) with the firm of surveyors for his own survey. They would receive this on top of the fee of £33 (£37.95 with VAT) for the building society valuation. He wrote confirming his instructions:

38 Broadstone Drive,
Hastings, Sussex.
23 May 1974.

Dear Sirs,
14 Twintree Avenue, Minford
I confirm my instructions, given on the telephone, that you should carry out a survey on the above property on my behalf.
We agreed that your fee would be £79.50 on the basis that you are also preparing

a valuation for the Forthright Building Society in connection with my purchase of this property. We further agreed that, as well as making the usual examination, you will examine and test the drains and the electrical system in the house. If it proves necessary to obtain the assistance of a plumber or an electrician, their charges will be in addition.

I further confirm that I hope to have your report within a fortnight.

Yours faithfully,
M. J. Seaton

Messrs. Andrew Robertson & Co.

DRAFT CONTRACT

A day or so later, Matthew received a letter from Dodds & Son, the firm of solicitors acting for Mr Timms, the seller:

Dodds & Son	*1 Charter Street,*
Solicitors	*Minford, Surrey.*
	23rd May, 1974.

Dear Sir,

14 Twintree Avenue, Minford

We understand that you propose purchasing the above-named property from our client, Mr W. H. Timms, at the price of £16250, subject to contract, and that you have paid a preliminary deposit of £100 to our client's agents, Messrs. Flint & Morgan. We further understand that you propose to act without a solicitor on the purchase.

We enclose the draft contract together with a copy for your use. Enclosed also is an extract from the Charges Register containing a copy of the restrictive covenants which affect the property.

Yours faithfully
Dodds & Son

M. J. Seaton, Esq.

The letter enclosed a draft of the contract. A contract is nearly always in a standard form and contains numerous printed clauses known as conditions of sale, which lay down the rights of the parties in almost every conceivable circumstance that might arise in the course of the transaction. There are two standard forms widely used by solicitors in England and Wales. One standard set of clauses is called the *National Conditions of Sale*; the other is called the *Law Society's Conditions of Sale*. Most solicitors have their own favourite of these two. There is an understanding between solicitors that the seller's solicitor decides which set of clauses—the National Conditions or the Law Society's Conditions—should apply in any one case. Of the two, the National Conditions are the more popular.

the National Conditions are the more popular

Both the National Conditions and the Law Society's Conditions are copyright, and the forms setting out the clauses cannot be bought by members of the public. At present, only solicitors may buy them.

Matthew was pleased that Dodds & Son had sent him a spare copy of the draft contract. It is the normal courtesy to send two copies of any document in draft to the other side. The recipient can then keep one copy for his own file, and send the other back with suggested amendments, if any. The draft contract was on the form which adopts the National Conditions of Sale, and not the one which adopts the Law Society's Conditions of Sale. It consisted of a piece of pale blue paper which folded down the middle to form four pages. On the inside two pages were set out the standard conditions, twenty-three of them, in small print. The front and the back were used to set out the details of the particular contract.

The front side of the contract was headed: 'CONTRACT by reference to the Nineteenth Edition of The National Conditions of Sale'. Under this heading were set out a series of panels in which the basic details of the proposed transaction had been completed. The full name, address and occupation of Mr Timms appeared in the space provided for 'Vendor', and corresponding details for Matthew appeared in the space for 'Purchaser'.

A small panel under the purchaser's name was headed Registered Land and Matthew needed to fill in the District Land Registry (Tunbridge Wells) and the title number: SY 43271604.

In the next panel, £16250 had been typed in by 'Purchase price'; below it was the heading 'Deposit'. It is normal practice for the buyer to pay 10 per cent of the purchase price to the seller's solicitors as a deposit. The buyer can demand to have it back at any time until the contract between buyer and seller is actually signed and exchanged. The buyer sometimes pays a smaller amount to the agents, as soon as the price is agreed, to show that he is serious in his intention of buying the property, the rest of the 10 per cent to be paid to the solicitors when contracts are exchanged.

It is normal for solicitors to hold the deposit as stakeholders. This means that they may not hand over to the seller the deposit, or any part of it, without the buyer's permission. The seller's solicitor may require that the deposit should be paid to him as 'agent for the vendor'. This means that the solicitor does not have to retain it until completion, and would have to pass it on, if asked to do so by the seller. The buyer should therefore insist that a solicitor, like an estate agent, should hold a deposit only as a stakeholder.

So far Matthew had only paid £100, he would therefore have to pay another £1525 when the contract became binding on him at exchange of contracts. This was likely to be in two or three weeks' time, and there was no point, he thought, in paying the full 10 per cent deposit until then.

Against 'price fixed for chattels' would be written the figure, if one had been agreed, which the buyer would be paying for items such as a lawn mower, or perhaps some furniture, such as a large wardrobe, that the seller was leaving behind, and the buyer would be buying. (It does not refer to fixtures and fittings, which are part of the house.)

Now came a panel in the contract form in which, under the heading 'Property and interest therein sold' there had been filled in a description of the property itself. The house was described in this way: *Freehold dwelling house and premises situate at and known as number 14, Twintree Avenue, Minford, Surrey.*

If the house had been a leasehold one, there would have been included here a reference to the lease: its date, who granted it originally and to whom, the period covered by the lease and the ground rent. The heading of this part of the form refers to 'the interest therein sold'. This means: is the property freehold or leasehold, and if leasehold, what are the particulars of the lease? In Matthew's case, the house was said to be freehold, and as this was what he had previously understood, this was acceptable.

The printed part of the contract then read: 'Vendor sells as . . .' and, in the space allowed, Dodds & Son had typed 'Beneficial Owner'. Mr Timms was specifically stated to be selling the house as beneficial owner. This meant that the property belonged to Mr Timms and the legal title to it was vested in him, too. Had the seller been the executor of a will and the house part of the estate, he would have sold as 'personal representative', instead of beneficial owner. Sometimes a house is owned by two or more people jointly, in which case they may be described as selling as 'trustees for sale'. Where the sellers are personal representatives, or husband and wife selling as trustees for sale, the buyer might be able to manage the transaction himself, but it will not be quite so straightforward as buying from an owner occupier who sells as beneficial owner. Very occasionally the capacity in which a seller sells is 'tenant for life'. In such a case the buyer should hesitate to deal with the matter without the help of a solicitor.

Next, the contract had a space for inserting the proposed completion date. The actual date was left blank at this stage. This date would have to be arranged when matters were a little more advanced. Matthew was quite anxious to move in as soon as possible, and had in mind that the date for completion should be about four weeks after exchange of contracts. Four weeks is about the time generally needed for what has to be done on the legal side between exchange of contracts and completion.

The bottom panel of the front of the contract form contained a brief statement of the gist of the whole document:

'AGREED that the vendor sells and the Purchaser buys as above, subject to the Special Conditions endorsed hereon and to the National Conditions of Sale Nineteenth Edition so far as the latter Conditions are not inconsistent with the Special Conditions'.

Immediately underneath was the space for signing the contract, when the time came, and for dating it. Matthew knew that he should not be tempted to write, in ink or ballpoint pen (pencil is all right because it can be rubbed out), on the spare copy of his contract, which Dodds and Son had sent to him. This spare copy would, eventually, if all went well, become the actual contract which he would exchange with the seller.

The rest of the contract form was devoted to the 'Special Conditions of Sale'. Here were typed the clauses for the contract which had been specifically included by Dodds & Son for this particular transaction. The first of these (Clause A) said 'The prescribed rate of interest is 14 per cent per annum above minimum lending rate. This covered the interest that the buyer has to pay if he completes the purchase later than the agreed date, or if he is allowed to take possession before completion. In either case the interest is calculated on the purchase price of the house, less the deposit. Sometimes the interest rate is a floating one, based on (but considerably above) the current bank lending rates. The next clause in the contract (Clause B) said that *the property is sold with vacant possession on completion*. This meant that the house would be completely empty when the time came, and no tenants or lodgers, or any refuse such as discarded furniture, would be there when Matthew came to move in. Matthew had in mind that he might want to take possession before completion if there was any delay, provided that Mr Timms agreed. He did not need to add anything to the clause to cover this; one of the standard conditions printed inside the form (condition 8) specifically set out the rights of buyer and seller should this happen.

Clause C of the special conditions of sale dealt with planning law, which does not allow changes, without planning consent, in the purpose for which property is used. Clause C said that the property was sold on the understanding that its currently permitted use was use as a dwellinghouse. This meant that so far as Mr Timms was concerned the property could be used only as a house: Matthew would be able to use it as a house and not as anything else, such as an office, or two flats. If Matthew wanted to give private tuition at the property, or turn it into two flats, or in any other way use it except as a dwellinghouse, he would have to make sure that he would get planning consent from the local council. But as Matthew had no thoughts of working from home, or of turning the house into two flats, or of doing anything with the property except live in the whole of it with his family, as Mr Timms had done, this clause was entirely acceptable to Matthew.

Clause D of the special conditions dealt with restrictive covenants. It read as follows:

'The property is sold subject to the covenants, conditions and stipulations contained in a Transfer dated the 14th day of June 1960 and made between Minford Estate Developments Limited ('the company') of the one part and Bernard Simon Isaacs of the other part. A copy of the said covenants, conditions and stipulations having been supplied to the purchaser, he shall be deemed to purchase with full knowledge thereof, and shall raise no requisition or enquiry with regard thereto.'

There had indeed been enclosed, with Dodds & Son's letter sending the draft contract, a copy of the restrictive covenants. This was a photocopy of part of the charges register relating to the property; part, that is, of the entries on the register. It read as follows:

'The following is a copy of the covenants contained in the Transfer dated 14 June 1960 mentioned in the Charges Register.
    'THE Purchaser hereby covenants with the Company and its successors in title and so that this covenant shall enure for the benefit of the remainder of the Company's estate at Minford in the County of Surrey

but so that he shall not be held liable after he shall have parted with all interest in the land at all times hereafter to observe and perform the restrictions stipulations and provisions set out in the Schedule hereto.

'The SCHEDULE above referred to

1. Not to erect any buildings on the land hereby transferred nor to alter raise or vary the elevation construction or height of the building already erected thereon except in accordance with plans elevations and specifications to be approved by the Company's architect or surveyor (such approval not to be unreasonably withheld) whose fee for perusing and approving such plans elevations and specifications shall be paid by the Purchaser.

2. No huts sheds caravans or temporary erections shall be placed or permitted on the said land or any part thereof except temporary erections to be used only for the works incidental to the erection of permanent buildings thereon.

3. No building of any description other than a boundary wall or bay windows or porches shall be erected on or over any part of the land hereby transferred nearer than 25 feet to the road fronting the said land.

4. Not to use or suffer to be used any buildings erected upon the said land or any part thereof for any purpose other than that of a private dwelling house and not to do or suffer thereon or on any part thereof or in any building thereon anything which shall be a nuisance or annoyance to the Company or its successors in title or to the neighbourhood.

5. No hoarding notice or advertisement shall at any time be erected or placed or suffered to be upon any part of the said property other than such as relates to the selling or letting of the dwellinghouse erected thereon'.

Not very easy reading perhaps, but worth careful study, Matthew thought. None of the covenants seemed likely to be troublesome. He had better check, he thought, that there had been no alteration or addition to the house since June 1960, when the covenants were imposed, which required the written permission of Minford Estate Developments Limited under the first of the covenants. He knew that an owner who puts up a greenhouse or adds a garage usually does not stop to think that there may be a restrictive covenant which demands written approval. Without such approval, the necessary consent has to be obtained when the property next comes to be sold. It is a seller's job to chase round and make whatever arrangements are necessary, and to pay any expenses involved in doing so. Matthew did not remember seeing anything built on the property which did not seem to have been there from the time when the house was built, but he decided to ask Dodds & Son about this, just to be sure.

That was the draft contract as it was received from Dodds & Son. Matthew noticed that it did not include a clause dealing with any fittings which the buyer might be taking over. A buyer is entitled to assume that anything—such as the boiler and the radiators in a central heating system—which is actually fixed (by screws or concrete for instance) to the property itself is a fixture, and so part of what he is buying, and automatically included in the price. It is essential for the parties to get quite clear between themselves exactly what is, and what is not, to be included in the price, and to make specific provision for it in the contract. There are nearly always some marginal items—light fittings, fitted cupboards, fixed appliances, a greenhouse or garden shed, even plants and shrubs in the garden—which could be the subject of dispute. The best plan is to agree whether they are included or not, and to say so in a clause in the contract.

Matthew remembered that when he and his wife had looked over the house, they had asked Mr Timms about the pelmets which were fitted more or less throughout the house. Mr Timms had assured them that the pelmets were included in the price. This had led to a discussion about other items which were included. It had been agreed that Mr Timms would throw in the staircarpet and the bathroom linoleum as well, both of which were somewhat worn, and hardly worth lifting. But Mr Timms had probably not told Dodds & Son, his solicitors, about this. Matthew decided that he should add a clause to the special conditions of sale to make it quite clear that the pelmets, bathroom linoleum and staircarpet were to be left behind and included in the price.

If the price of a house is just a little over £15000, say £15200, it is quite legitimate, for the buyer and seller, to sell separately any articles which were intended to be included, so as to bring the price for the house below £15000. If this is done, there will be no stamp duty for the buyer to pay on the transfer, as this bears stamp duty only where the price exceeds £15000. If, for example, a sale is so arranged in good faith that a price of £15100, including curtains, carpets and gas stove, becomes a price of £14900, and a separate sale is made under which the curtains, carpets and gas stove are sold for £200, the buyer will save £75.50 in stamp duty. A similar saving can be made where the price narrowly exceeds £20000 or £25000 or £30000, where the rates of stamp duty jump from a lower rate to a higher rate. Stamp duty can be saved in this way only where the price is genuinely arranged before the contract becomes binding, and only where it can honestly be said that the price for the fittings bears a reasonable approximation to their real value.

If Dodds & Son had used the Law Society's Conditions of Sale instead of the National Conditions, Matthew would have received a similar draft contract, but set out differently. Sometimes a solicitor uses a form he has prepared himself which will incorporate, by reference, the clauses from one of the two standard sets of conditions.

Before Matthew could tell Dodds & Son whether he approved the draft contract, he would need to have the answers from them to a number of questions, which he would ask them in his formal enquiries before contract.

ENQUIRIES BEFORE CONTRACT

Matthew now needed the first of the forms he had bought, the form of 'Enquiries before contract' to be sent to Dodds & Son, the seller's solicitor. Enquiries before contract—otherwise known as preliminary enquiries—is a list of questions about the property which is sent to the seller's solicitor. The majority of solicitors use the printed forms of 'Enquiries before contract' (Conveyancing 29 Long). Questions which it has been found a buyer needs to ask of a seller are printed on the lefthand side of the form, with spaces for the answers.

The first fifteen questions under the heading 'General enquiries' apply to all cases and deal with such subjects as ownership of boundaries, disputes (with neighbours, for instance), main services (water, gas and electricity), rights of way and similar rights, restrictive covenants, planning, fixtures and fittings, roads, outgoings other than rates, rateable value, and when completion can be expected.

The fifteenth question on the form, headed 'new properties' only applies to newly built houses and covers some of the particular problems that apply in such cases.

The back page of the form applies to leasehold property. The questions deal with: whether the lease is a head lease (one where the landlord is the freeholder), or an underlease (one where the landlord also holds the property under a lease, a superior lease, as it is called); the name and address of the present landlord, the landlord of any superior lease, their respective solicitors, and the agents (if any) to whom the ground rent is paid; whether the requirements of the lease about painting and doing other work to the property have been honoured; and details of insurance, which, under the terms of the lease, often has to be placed with a particular insurance company.

The rest of the back page is left blank for any additional questions. In the case of a straightforward sale of an owner occupied house which has a registered title, it is quite common to find no extra questions. In less simple cases, points nearly always occur to the buyer's solicitor on which he requires information or assurance. This is so, even though the ground is very well covered by the printed questions in the rest of the form.

At the top of the form of enquiries before contract, Matthew wrote 14 Twintree Avenue, Minford. Underneath there was a space for writing the names of the seller and of the buyer. Matthew needed Dodds & Son's answers to all but the last two of the 15 general enquiries in the form; they were asked automatically without adding anything to the form. Matthew struck out the last two and all the rest of the printed enquiries, which only applied if the property was leasehold and 14 Twintree Avenue was not. On the back of the form was a space for any questions that the buyer wanted to ask in addition to the printed ones. Matthew thought of two. Firstly: 'Since 14 June 1960, has any alteration or addition been made to the house which required consent under covenant number 1 in the schedule to the transfer of that date? If so, please confirm that any necessary consent has been obtained and will be handed over on completion.'

This arose out of the restrictive covenant which required the consent of the original developers, Minford Estate Developments Limited, before any alterations or additions could be made. Matthew was anxious not to be in a position where he would himself have to apply for approval of something which Mr Timms, or perhaps his predecessor, had done to the property. Worse still, he did not want to have to restore the property to its original condition. Hence the question.

Matthew's second addition was: 'Please send a copy of the filed plan'. He needed this in order to check that the Land Registry plan tallied with the property itself in all respects.

He signed and dated the form of the enquiries before contract and sent it, in duplicate, to Dodds & Son with this letter:

38 Broadstone Drive,
Hastings, Sussex.
29 May 1974.

Dear Sirs,

14 Twintree Avenue, Minford

Thank you for your letter of 23 May 1974 enclosing the draft contract relating to my proposed purchase of the above property. I am grateful for the copy for my use.
▪I enclose some preliminary enquiries, with a copy.

Yours faithfully,

M. J. Seaton

Messrs. Dodds & Son
1, Charter Street,
Minford, Surrey.

LOCAL SEARCHES

At the same time, Matthew prepared and sent off applications for local searches and also enquiries to the local authorities. A local search is an application for a certificate to state whether the local authority, or other official body, has recorded any specific claim or restriction against the property. The buyer hopes to find no adverse claims, officially known as 'local land charges', registered in the local land charges register. But there may, for instance, be an outstanding claim for unpaid road charges, or it may be that a sanitary notice was served on the occupier because of some defect in the drains. The local search reveals these matters. Sometimes the local search reveals details of planning schemes which may sooner or later have an effect on the property. These need to be investigated, so that the buyer knows what the official short and long term planning position is likely to be. There is no formal way of finding out what plans there may be at the formative stage which are not yet officially revealed.

A local search is made with the local district council. In Matthew's case it was Minford District Council. In London, the search is made with the appropriate borough council.

Matthew used form LLC1 (requisition for search in the register of local land charges), for his search with Minford District Council. He wrote the name of the council in the space near the top of the form: Minford DC. Form LLC1 has a printed duplicate of itself attached, to be torn off and retained by the local council, the original only being sent back with the signed certificate on it. Both parts have to be filled in when applying, and this is most easily done by using carbon paper.

The register of local land charges is divided into twelve parts and it is possible for a buyer to apply for a search in just those parts with which he is concerned. But the almost universal practice is to apply for a search of the whole local register, and this is what Matthew did. To achieve this, Matthew crossed out the words '*Parts . . . . . . .of*' on the form to make it read: '*An official search is required in the register of local land charges*'. A search certificate will only speak as to the state of affairs on the day of its date. It could happen that, on the day after it is issued, some fundamental change takes place which alters the whole picture as shown in the search certificate. Where a person is buying a house, the buyer is usually anxious to receive the search certificate as soon as possible.

In filling in the form, it is seldom necessary to do more than describe the property (referred to in the form as the 'land') by its ordinary address. For instance, 14 Twintree Avenue, Minford, Surrey was sufficient in Matthew's case. Occasionally, it is impossible to identify a property sufficiently by a mere description. In such a case it is necessary to send a plan.

Matthew signed the form, dated it and wrote his name, address and phone number in the panel provided. The cost of obtaining a local search certificate is £1·25.

With form LLC1 Matthew sent an application for answers to a number of additional enquiries, on a form called 'Enquiries of District Councils'. This is a printed form on which the buyer asks the local authority for a good deal more information than is revealed by the official local search alone. Among the items which are covered by this form are: roads, main services, planning, and rent control.

There are two different editions of this form for use with the different sorts of local authority. If the house is in the area of a district council, the enquiries of local authority are made on form Con. 29, England and Wales.

For a house in the Greater London area, the search must be with the appropriate London borough council. The form of additional enquiries for London is Con. 29 London.

The form of enquiries is divided into two parts. All the questions in part I will be automatically answered; a question in part II, however, is only answered if the enquirer indicates, by placing his initials alongside the question, that he wants to have an answer. It is unusual for a buyer of a second-hand house to need to ask any part II questions.

The cost of replies to enquiries of local authority is £4·50, which must be paid in addition to the £1·25 charged for the search certificate.

Matthew sent both forms to Minford District Council at the council offices, Minford. He enclosed the cheque, payable to the council, for £5·75. Matthew hoped to receive back his local search certificate and replies to enquiries within a week or two of sending off the forms.

REPLIES TO ENQUIRIES BEFORE CONTRACT

Dodds & Son sent back Matthew's enquiries before contract with their replies more or less by return of post:

Dodds & Son   *1 Charter Street,*
  Solicitors   *Minford, Surrey.*
                                                     31st May, 1974.

Dear Sir,

14, Twintree Avenue, Minford

We enclose our answers to your preliminary enquiries and look forward to hearing from you with the draft contract duly approved as soon as possible.

Yours faithfully,
Dodds & Son

M. J. Seaton, Esq.

The answers, typed in the spaces provided on the form of enquiries before contract, were much as Matthew would have expected. Solicitors have a technique for answering preliminary enquiries. Just as there are stock questions, so are there stock answers which crop up frequently. Among these answers are: 'Inspection will show'; 'Please search'; 'Other than those apparent on inspection or revealed by the usual searches and enquiries, there are none to the vendor's knowledge'; and 'We cannot say'. A liberal sprinkling of such noncommittal replies, together with guarded but positive replies to such questions as the seller's solicitor is able to answer informatively, may be all that can be expected.

Many of the printed questions sought a positive assurance that there were no adverse rights or interests which affected some specific aspect of 14 Twintree Avenue. The answer to these was usually: 'There are none of which the vendor is aware but the property is sold subject to any there may be'.

The first question concerned ownership of walls, fences and hedges; the answer referred to the plan drawn at the time when the house was first built. Where a line on a plan indicates a boundary between two properties, it is a common practice to show a T mark on one side of the line. This shows that this particular fence or hedge belongs to the owner of the property inside which the T mark appears. By referring to the plan on which the T marks appeared, a copy of which Dodds & Son sent with their replies, Matthew was able to tell which fences were his and which were his neighbours'. Although two of the fences appeared to belong to 14 Twintree Avenue, there was nothing to say that he would be obliged to maintain them. Sometimes there is a covenant about maintaining boundary fences.

There was none in this case. This meant that Matthew could not be forced to maintain the fences if he did not want to; it also meant, probably, that if the fence on the other side of the garden, which by inference belonged to the neighbour on that side, fell down or needed repair, Matthew would be unable to force the neighbour to repair it. Ownership of fences is one thing; obligation to repair is another.

After questions about disputes and notices (there were none), there was a question about guarantees. This referred to things such as the certificate issued by the National House-Building Council for houses built under their scheme, or woodworm treatment guarantees, or agreements regarding footpaths. A buyer should be concerned to get the benefit of any such guarantees. Information about them is requested now, so that after exchange of contracts they can be transferred to the new owner. This can be by a simple letter from the seller to the buyer, saying "In consideration of your completing your purchase of my house, I now assign to you the benefit of the guarantee dated XYZ which I received from So-and-so regarding this-and-that." A copy of the letter of assignment should be sent to the people who gave the guarantee.

There were questions about gas, electricity, drainage and other main services (they were connected); and whether any exclusive or shared facilities, adverse rights or arrangements affected the property. Matthew was reassured to find that there were, so far as was known, none of which he was previously unaware. He was told that, so far as the seller knew, the restrictive covenants had all been honoured and that any consents required by any covenants had been obtained.

Now followed a multiple question, dealing with many aspects of planning. It asked since when the property had had its present use, and whether that use was continuous. The answer confirmed that the property had been continuously used, since 1960, as a private dwelling house. It was consistent with the clause in the special conditions of sale in the draft contract. All was well: Matthew intended to go on using it as a house.

Then it asked whether any building had been carried out on the property in the previous four years. In the case of Twintree Avenue, Matthew had understood that the house had been built in about 1960, more than four years previously. According to the current conveyancing practice, therefore, he did not need to investigate further the planning consent that had then been obtained.

The house had every appearance of having been one of a whole estate built at the same time, and it was highly unlikely that planning permission had not been obtained. It might have been different had the house been on a site by itself, instead of on an estate, or if it had filled a gap between two other houses of long standing. In that case, the planning permission would have related to the building of just the one house and should have been kept, and would eventually be handed over to Matthew. He decided to ask for confirmation that planning permission had been obtained, during the visit he intended shortly to make to the planning department at Minford DC offices.

Another answer revealed that the fixtures and fittings would be part of the sale. The question referred also specifically to trees, shrubs, plants, flowers and garden produce.

Another question asked for the rateable value of the property and whether any works had been carried out which might increase this. And the next question asked about completion and when vacant possession would be given. The answer was: four weeks after exchange of contracts.

The fifteenth question in the first section of the form concerned new properties—those being built, or just built. In Matthew's case, it was crossed out.

The next part of the form applied only to leasehold property. For such cases, information would be obtained about matters such as whether the lease was a head lease (where the landlord owns the freehold) or an underlease (where the landlord also has a lease); the name and address of the landlord (referred to as the lessors) and his agents and solicitors; whether the obligations in the lease—about painting and repairing the property, for instance—had been fulfilled by the tenant; details of service charges for the last three years (for maintaining the roof of a block of flats, for instance); particulars of the insurance policy; and particulars (available in the case of some long leases) of the landlord's title to the property, which can act as an added safeguard against trouble from someone with whom the landlord might have had a quarrel regarding his rights in the property.

The questions covered a great variety of topics, and the answers were often far from specific. Solicitors are even more chary about giving direct answers to preliminary enquiries than they were before 1967, when a new law was introduced on the subject of misrepresentations. This makes a seller legally responsible for the accuracy of information given before a contract is signed. While this is, of course, a good thing, it may tend to reduce the clarity with which answers to preliminary enquiries are given.

All answers to the printed questions were satisfactory, and the only other questions that had to be answered were the two that Matthew had added. One had asked whether there had been any alteration or addition to the property since the house was built. This question was really supplementary to the printed questions about restrictions and consents. It was asking, in more precise terms, whether there had been any breach of the restrictive covenant which demanded the consent of the original developer to any alterations and additions to the house. Dodds & Son answered in the usual non-committal way: 'The vendor knows of no alteration or addition which required consent under that covenant'.

The other had asked for a copy of the filed plan. 'Herewith' was the answer and a copy of the plan was indeed enclosed. The plan looked all right, but Matthew decided to take it with him when he and his wife would visit the house again shortly, just to make sure that the plan tallied in all respects with the property itself.

Matthew was satisfied with the answers he had received to his preliminary enquiries, even though some of the answers were somewhat guarded. He could now move to the next stage.

APPROVAL OF DRAFT CONTRACT

Matthew was ready to return the draft contract to Dodds & Son, now that he had satisfactory replies to his preliminary enquiries. He remembered to add a clause to the draft contract which would deal with the pelmets, the bathroom lino and staircarpet, the items which Mr Timms had said he would throw in.

The custom between solicitors is that amendments to draft documents should appear in various coloured inks, red first, then green and so on. Thus the buyer's solicitor, if he wishes to suggest some alterations to the draft contract, makes them in red ink, and, retaining one copy with the alterations on it for his own file, sends the other copy, with the red alterations on it, back to the seller's solicitor. If the seller's solicitor is unable to agreed the amendments, he either alters the draft back to its original form, or suggests some other amendment, a compromise perhaps. This he does in green ink. It can happen that a draft document goes backwards and forwards between solicitors for quite a long time, gradually getting more and more colourful. Eventually negotiations will either be called off, or the parties will agree terms. But for a simple case of a house with a registered title, it is unlikely that it will be necessary to go beyond one set of amendments before terms are agreed.

. . . getting more and more colourful . . .

Matthew found a red ballpoint pen and wrote (as special condition D) on the top copy of the draft contract (but in pencil on his second copy) a new clause: 'The following items are declared to be included in the price: pelmets in all rooms, linoleum in bathroom, and staircarpet'. If Dodds & Son had, contrary to the normal practice, sent Matthew only one copy of the draft contract in the first instance, Matthew would have kept it, and dealt with the suggested amendment in a letter. But as they had sent him the usual two copies, he amended the top copy in red (keeping the carbon copy, amended in pencil, for himself), and wrote:

> *38 Broadstone Drive,*
> *Hastings, Sussex.*
> *2 June 1974.*

Dear Sirs,

14 Twintree Avenue, Minford

Thank you for your letter of 31 May. I now return the draft contract which I approve, subject to satisfactory local searches and subject to one addition, which is written on the draft in red. When I have received back my local searches and heard from my proposed mortgagees, I shall then be ready to exchange contracts.

I have discussed with your client the question of completion; we have provisionally agreed that I shall be able to move in on friday, 26 July.

> *Yours faithfully,*
> *M. J. Seaton*

Messrs. Dodds & Son

The second paragraph of this letter referred to a telephone conversation which Mr Timms had had with Matthew on the question of moving day. They would need, Matthew reckoned, at least six more weeks to deal with the legal formalities. On that basis, 26 July was not to optimistic, and was a date to aim for.

LOCAL SEARCH CERTIFICATES

Two days later Matthew received the local search certificate from Minford DC. With it, he received the replies of the local authority to the questions asked on form Con. 29A (England and Wales). The search certificate revealed that there were matters affecting 14 Twintree Avenue in the register of local land charges: these consisted of 'the two entries described in the Schedule hereto'.

Matthew considered the attached schedule and found that there was nothing to worry about on account of what was there revealed. The schedule merely contained a long-winded reference to the old pre-1947 planning legislation, under which there had, apparently, been planning schemes set on foot in the 1930s. These old schemes, nowadays usually overtaken by more up to date development plans, often reveal themselves in official searches in the local land charges register. Solicitors usually do not have any qualms about them when they turn up.

The answers from Minford DC to the enquiries made on form Con. 29A were standardised: Minford DC had replied by supplying a typed list of answers. Matthew went through the answers carefully. The answers confirmed that all was well. They revealed that Twintree Avenue was maintained at public expense, so that Matthew would not be faced with having to pay road charges; no road widening plans were likely to affect the property; there were no proposals on foot to build a new road near the property; no sanitary or similar notices were outstanding in respect of the property; the property drained into a public sewer. There had been no infringement of the building regulations nor of the planning legislation (which was what the enforcement notice under the Town and Country Planning Acts referred to). The development plan for the district did not designate the property as being liable to compulsory purchase, and the area of Twintree Avenue was regarded primarily as a residential one. Minford DC kept a list of planning permissions granted in respect of the property (that is the register kept under section 34 of the Town and Country Planning Act 1971); and details of the planning consent regarding the original development in 1958 were given. Every property has a register of planning permissions kept for it, either with the district council or with the county council. The answers to the respective questions on the forms about the register should show which council it is in any particular case.

The answers supplied by Minford DC were quite comprehensible, and Matthew realised that he was not really overwhelmed by all the legal verbiage. He knew that if there was anything which he did not understand, like a firm proposal for compulsory purchase, he could telephone or visit the department of the council which issued it and ask for clarification. If there is something on the searches or enquiries which cannot be resolved by doing that, the buyer would have to consult a solicitor.

MORTGAGE OFFER

The purchase now started moving forward on another front. Matthew received a letter from the Forthright Building Society:

Forthright Building Society   88 *Lomax Street,*
Minford, Surrey.
5th June, 1974.

Dear Sir,

14 Twintree Avenue, Minford

The Society has now received the report of its surveyor regarding the above property and is able to offer you an advance in the sum of £13000 to be secured by a mortgage on the above property. The loan is conditional upon its being taken up within three months of this date.

I enclose details of the proposed loan on our formal notification, from which you will see that the interest rate will be 11 per cent per annum at first, but the Society reserves the right to alter the interest rate on giving 3 months' notice. The loan will be repayable over a 25 year period, by monthly instalments of £129.

The solicitors who will act for the Society in connection with the legal formalities of the mortgage will be Messrs. Hodgson, Green & Co., of this town, who will be getting in touch with you shortly.

Yours faithfully,
M. C. Templeton
Manager

M. J. Seaton, Esq.

The enclosed notification and acceptance form was in these terms:

Forthright Building Society
Head Office: Forthright House,
Somerset Square,
London, E.C.3.

Please reply to:
88 Lomax Street,
Minford, Surrey.
5th June 1974.

Offer of Advance
re: *14 Twintree Avenue, Minford*

Forthright Building Society offers to advance you the sum mentioned below, such sum to be secured on the above property, upon these terms and conditions:

1. The property is Freehold/~~Leasehold with~~......................~~years to run.~~
2. The offer is subject to the Society being finally satisfied as to your financial position and prospects.
3. Amount to be advanced *£13000* repayable by monthly payments of *£129* each over a period of *25* years. Each payment includes a proportion of principal and of interest.
4. Interest rate *11* per cent per annum. The right is reserved to vary this rate of interest on giving three months' notice to do so. Effect may be given to variations in the interest rate by increasing or decreasing the period over which the payments are made (see Para 3 above). Interest is calculated annually on the amount of the loan outstanding at 31st December in each year.
5. The property must throughout the period of the loan remain insured against fire and other risks in a sum of not less than its full value; this at first is *£16250*. The insurance will be arranged with a company approved by the Society.
6. The legal formalities in connection with the mortgage will be dealt with on behalf of the Society by the Society's solicitors *Messrs. Hodgson Green & Co of 67 Lomax Street, Minford, Surrey*. Their fees and disbursements are payable by you, and are deducted from the loan when it is made. The loan is conditional upon the Society's solicitors being satisfied regarding the property's title and otherwise.
7. ~~The repairs listed in the accompanying schedule must be effected before completion/within~~ ....~~months of completion.~~
8. The property must not be let in any way nor may alterations or additions be made to it without the Society's written consent, to be obtained in advance.
9. The Society reserves the right to modify or withdraw this offer at any time until the loan is effected.

To: *Matthew J. Seaton, Esq.*   G. Percy Marshall
    38 Broadstone Drive, Hastings, Sussex.   Advance Manager

An advance of £13000 was what Matthew had applied for, and this had been granted. It was quite normal to find that a loan has to be taken up within three months, otherwise the offer to lend the money lapses. You cannot expect a building society to be left wondering indefinitely whether the matter is to go ahead or not. In practice, however, a building society is often willing to extend the time limit, if a delay is explained.

Matthew was not surprised to find that he would have to pay the legal costs of the building society's solicitors, Hodgson Green & Co. This is normal practice. It was probable that this firm acted generally for the Minford branch of the building society. There are some building societies, particularly the bigger ones, which adopt the panel system, whereby many solicitors all over the country are on the panel of solicitors who could act for them. In this way, it often happens that the same solicitor acts for the buyer and for the building society, with a saving in legal expense to the buyer as a result.

Clause 8 showed that, strictly speaking, no lettings or alterations could be made without the building society's consent.

There was nothing binding—either on the building society or on Matthew—about the offer of a mortgage: clause 9 of the official notification made this clear. A building society rarely commits itself in advance to making a loan so that, theoretically at least, the buyer of a house may be placed in a vulnerable position. He has to commit himself to the seller by a binding contract and does this on the strength of an offer—but not a binding one—from a building society to lend him part of the purchase price. If, for some reason—such as that his financial circumstances had taken a turn for the worse—the building society were to back out before the loan was made, or, in an economic crisis, the proposed interest rate was increased, the buyer could do nothing about it.

The form from the Forthright Building Society was in duplicate, an original and a tear-off copy. A notice on the back of the form from the building society, referring to section 30 of the Building Societies Act 1962, said that the society did not warrant that the purchase price of the property was reasonable. This was a formality which the society put in to cover itself on this question, and is quite normal.

The terms of the offer were as Matthew had expected and he felt able to sign the form of acceptance.

ACCEPTANCE   *6 June, 1974*
I, *Matthew J. Seaton* of *38 Broadstone Drive, Hastings, Sussex,* accept your
offer to make an advance to be secured on *14 Twintree Avenue, Minford,
Surrey,* upon the terms and conditions made known to me.

My solicitors are ....

Signed: *M. J. Seaton*

To: Forthright Building Society.

The acceptance, which Matthew had to sign and return to the society,
was appended to the bottom of the copy. He sent the following letter with
it:

> *38 Broadstone Drive,*
> *Hastings, Sussex.*
> *6 June 1974.*

Dear Sir,
> *14 Twintree Avenue, Minford*
*I thank you for your letter of 5 June and its enclosure, from which I am pleased
to learn that you are willing to grant me a mortgage loan to be secured on the above.
I note the terms of the advance, and look forward to hearing from your solicitors.
I return the acceptance form, which I have signed.*
> *Yours faithfully,*
> *M. J. Seaton*

The Manager,
Forthright Building Society,
Minford, Surrey.

He heard again from Dodds & Son:

Dodds & Son   *1 Charter Street,*
Solicitors   *Minford, Surrey,*
                                                      7th June, 1974.
Dear Sir,
                    14 Twintree Avenue, Minford
   We thank you for your letter of the 2nd June, returning the draft contract. Your
amendments in red are approved and we are engrossing the contract. No doubt you
will let us have the contract duly signed as soon as possible. We confirm that the
completion date should be 26th July, 1974 and have inserted that date in the contract.
                           Yours faithfully,
                           Dodds & Son
M. J. Seaton, Esq.

   This letter did not commit Mr Timms, the seller, to signing the contract
as amended by Matthew. All it implied was: 'We anticipate that the seller
will be prepared to sign a contract so worded, when the time comes'.
   When the wording of the contract is agreed, each side prepares a fair
copy of it which each will sign; lawyers call it the engrossment. If the
contract is approved as originally drafted, or with only minor variations,
each side will probably use the draft contract itself as the engrossment.
   Matthew had been careful to write his suggested amendment to the draft
contract (the addition of the new clause) in pencil on his copy of the form
of the National Conditions of Sale. By doing so, he was able to use this
form as the engrossment itself. To the layman, unable to buy the form of
the National Conditions of Sale, which is sold only to solicitors, the best
course is to preserve the original draft contract, and make separate or
pencilled notes of the alterations, as they are suggested. Then the alterations, if any, needed to produce the final form of the contract can be added
when they are all agreed, and that can constitute the engrossment for
signature.

VISIT TO THE LOCAL COUNCIL
Matthew wanted more information than that revealed by his local search
and enquiries. These had given him a pretty good idea so far as 14 Twintree
Avenue itself was concerned, but only a vague idea of the probable
development pattern in the coming years in Minford as a whole. If this
town was to be their home for an unknown period of years in the future,
it was important, he thought, to get the feel of probable future development
in the area. This merited a visit to the planning department of Minford
district council.

He found the people in the planning department helpful, and glad to explain the local planning situation to him. They showed him the development plan, a large scale map of the district with different areas shaded different colours. One colour showed the parts of the district which were intended for residential use, another colour showed the parts intended for shops and offices, another the light industrial areas, and further colours showed open spaces, positions for schools, and areas which were to be kept—it was hoped—in the green belt. So far as Matthew could judge, nothing that was planned was likely drastically to affect 14 Twintree Avenue. He noted that a new secondary school was planned for a large open space on the edge of the green belt quite near Twintree Avenue, which might make some differences to them, and at least it would be less far for the children to go to school. He asked to see, and was shown, the plans for this school, the building of which was to begin the next year. There were plans for two new housing estates on the other side of town, and ultimately—five years hence was probably the earliest—a by-pass was to be built.

While he was at the council offices, he took the opportunity of referring to the local search certificate and to the answers to the enquiries asked of Minford DC. He asked to see the register of planning applications made for 14 Twintree Avenue—the register kept under section 34 of the Town and Country Planning Act, as the question on form Con. 29A had described it. This showed that planning permission had been given to Minford Estate Developments Limited in 1958 to build the estate of houses which now included 14 Twintree Avenue. By looking at the plans for the estate which the council had approved. Matthew was able to identify 14 Twintree Avenue and to check that the house as built was the same as that for which permission had been given. He came away with a much better idea about the locality, present and future.

LOOKING AT THE HOUSE

While in Minford, he went to 14 Twintree Avenue with a copy of the filed plan sent to him by Dodds & Son. He compared the plan with the actual property, to see whether the plan was correct, and that there was nothing on the property which could be the cause of confusion or disputes with neighbours in the future. It is always as well for the buyer to compare the particulars in the contract and the plan with the actual property, to make sure that they correspond. If they do not, a buyer should raise the question with the seller, and if necesary take legal advice.

The next letter to arrive was from the solicitors acting for the Forthright Building Society:

Hodgson, Green & Co.   *67 Lomax Street,*
Solicitors   *Minford, Surrey.*
                                                            12th June, 1974.
Dear Sir,
                       14 Twintree Avenue, Minford
  Our clients, Forthright Building Society, have instructed us with regard to an advance on mortgage of £13000 to be made to you and to be secured on the above property. We understand that you will be acting for yourself in this matter.
  When the legal formalities regarding your purchase are sufficiently advanced, please let us have the following documents: Contract, Preliminary Enquiries & replies, local Searches, office copy of the entries on the Register and filed plan, authority for us to inspect the Register, Requisitions on Title and replies, and draft Transfer as approved by the vendor's Solicitors.
                          Yours faithfully,
                        Hodgson, Green & Co.
Matthew J. Seaton, Esq.

Nothing unexpected there. Apart from a routine acknowledgment, no further action was needed with Hodgson, Green & Co. until after exchange of contracts.

Matthew had not yet heard from Andrew Robertson & Co. with their report on the survey they had carried out for him. He knew that they had inspected the property because the Forthright Building Society would not have made the mortgage offer without their valuation. He gave them a ring to prod them into action, and learnt that his report was in draft and would be ready shortly.

INSURANCE

A buyer should insure his property for risks, such as fire, storm, flood, damage by burglars, and to cover the owner's liability for accidents caused by the building, such as by a roof-tile falling down. The type of policy which the buyer and building society need is a household buildings policy, called different names by different insurance companies.

A buyer might be forgiven for thinking that this is something he need not worry about until his purchase is completed, and that, if the property was damaged before completion, the seller's insurance would take care of it. This is not necessarily so. Once contracts have been exchanged between buyer and seller, the property is at the buyer's risk, and if any disaster befalls the house between the time of exchanging contracts and completion, the buyer still has to go through with the purchase, and nobody else will pay for the cost of repairs. So the buyer should make sure that he is covered for insurance from the moment he exchanges contracts.

As well as the present owner and prospective buyer, the building society has a very strong vested interest in the insurance. If the house were burnt down and there were no insurance, most of the security for the loan would have gone up in smoke. To be on the safe side, the building society insists that the policy is with an insurance company it knows well, and that the policy has a note of the mortgage endorsed on it.

It has now become universal practice for building societies to handle the entire business of insurance for the buyer, through special block policies they hold the with the insurance companies. It is then only necessary for the buyer to satisfy himself that the sum insured is, in his view, adequate to cover the cost of wholly rebuilding the property after a total loss including about 15 per cent for architects' and surveyors' fees and the cost of clearing the site of debris in the case of total destruction.

On Matthew's mortgage application form from the Forthright Building Society, there was a section about insurance. The Forthright had suggested that his insurance should be with the Bridstow Insurance Company Limited, but a borrower is entitled to choose from three companies approved by the building society. The Bridstow Insurance Company had a local office in Guildford. There was no need or opportunity for Matthew to fill in a proposal form himself and send it off to the insurance company—the building society would see to that side of things for him. And where building societies have block policies with insurance companies, the buyer does not even get his own copy of the insurance policy. If he wants to find out about the details, he must ask his building society.

Matthew knew that a building society often pays the first premium to make sure that the insurance is effective, and deducts the amount from the loan to the buyer. Similarly, some building societies also pay the subsequent insurance premiums and add the amount each year to one of the monthly mortgage payments. Eventually the building society would notify Matthew how much his premium was based on how much the house was insured for.

There can be quite a difference between the market value of a house (how much the buyer pays) and its reinstatement value (how much an identical house would cost to rebuild). This is always higher than the market value, and it is on this amount that the building society takes out insurance, not on the amount of the mortgage loan.

It is quite likely that the building society will look after a buildings policy only, and the buyer must make sure that contents insurance starts as soon as there is any of his own property inside the house. This may be before moving day if there is an agreement between the seller and buyer that certain items will be left inside the house. It is sensible to take out a house contents policy with the same company with which the building is insured.

written in the mournful language of surveyors

SURVEYOR'S REPORT

Matthew next received the surveyor's report. It was written in the mournful language of surveyors. The gist of it was that the house was structurally sound, but full of petty faults which were largely design errors and could not now be rectified. There were some loose tiles on the roof and some cracks needed making good. Apart from this, the house was in good order. There was nothing in the surveyor's report to deter Matthew and there was no specific item sufficient to justify his suggesting to Mr Timms that, because of it, the price might be lowered. The agreed price of £16250 had, up till then, been 'subject to survey'.

He now wrote to the insurance company:

38, Broadstone Drive,
Hastings, Sussex.
20 June 1974.

Dear Sirs.

14 Twintree Avenue, Minford

As I understand the Forthright Building Society is taking out insurance cover for my new property with you, I should be grateful if you would send me a proposal form for contents insurance, to start from the date of completion 26th July.

Yours faithfully,
M. J. Seaton

Bridstow Insurance Co. Ltd.

Matthew felt that as Mr Timms was not leaving any valuables behind, he would not bother to insure the contents until his own furniture and belongings were moved in. He had asked the Forthright Building Society to let him have a copy of the buildings insurance policy.

EXCHANGE OF CONTRACTS

The buyer signs only one engrossment of the contract and expects to receive in exchange a similar engrossment signed only by the seller.

the buyer jumps first

The tradition is that the buyer jumps first. The buyer's solicitor sends the part of the contract signed by the buyer to the seller's solicitor, on condition that in exchange the seller's solicitor sends him the part of the contract signed by the seller. This is the exchange of contracts. It is usually done by post, but where both sides are in the same town, it might be done in person. The seller's solicitor is usually left to fill in the date on both parts of the contract. This date is usually the day on which he sends off the part signed by his client, the seller. There is usually no legally binding contract between the parties until the seller's solicitor has posted the contract signed by the seller. At that moment both buyer and seller are legally bound to go through with the transaction. The buyer must now pay the whole of the deposit, or the balance of the deposit.

Matthew Seaton was now ready to send off to Dodds & Son, solicitors for the owner Mr W. H. Timms, the contract to buy 14 Twintree Avenue, Minford, and so commit himself to go through with the deal. This was because:
1. the form and the wording of the contract had been agreed;
2. the replies he had received to his enquiries before contract had been satisfactory;
3. the local search certificate and replies to enquiries made of the local authority were satisfactory;
4. he had made firm arrangements to borrow on mortgage the amount he needed;
5. arrangements had been made for the property to be insured;
6. he had received a satisfactory report from a surveyor.

He sent the contract to Dodds & Son with this letter:

38 Broadstone Drive,
Hastings, Sussex.
21 June 1974.

Dear Sirs,

14 Twintree Avenue, Minford

I now enclose the contract signed by me. Please date it. I have inserted 26 July as the date for completion, as agreed with Mr Timms.

Flint and Morgan hold a preliminary deposit of £100, and I now enclose my cheque for £1525, the balance of the deposit (10 per cent of the price).

I look forward to receiving from you as soon as possible the contract signed by your client, together with copy entries on the register and authority to inspect the register.

Yours faithfully,
M. J. Seaton

Messrs. Dodds & Son.

If Matthew had not had enough money to pay the deposit, he would have had to make financial arrangements with his bank for a bridging loan. This can be an expensive exercise.

He now heard from the insurance company:

Bridstow Insurance Co. Ltd.　　　　　　　　　　　　*403, High Street,*
Guildford, Surrey
21st June, 1974.

Dear Sir,

re 14 Twintree Avenue, Minford

Thank you for your letter of yesterday's date.

We have pleasure in enclosing the proposal form you requested.

We note what you say about the date of commencement of cover, and, on receipt of the requisite premium, shall be pleased to let you have the same.

Assuring you of our best attention at all times.

Your faithfully,
for and on behalf of
Bridstow Insurance Co. Ltd.
H. G. Mason
for Manager

M. J. Seaton, Esq.

—and soon afterwards from Dodds & Son:

Dodds & Son   *1 Charter Street,*
Solicitors   *Minford, Surrey.*
                                                          24th June, 1974.
Dear Sir,
                    14 Twintree Avenue, Minford
   We thank you for your letter of 21st instant enclosing contract duly signed, together
with your cheque for the balance of the deposit.
   We now have pleasure in enclosing the part of the contract signed by our client,
Mr Timms. We have dated both parts of the contract with today's date, and confirm
that the date for completion is fixed by the contract at 26th July, 1974.
   We enclose an authority for you to inspect the Register.
            We look forward to hearing further from you in due course.
                         Yours faithfully,
                         Dodds & Son
M. J. Seaton, Esq.

The contract they sent was an exact counterpart of the one Matthew had
signed and sent off, but was signed by Mr Timms. Thus contracts were
exchanged; neither could back out now.

ENTRIES ON REGISTER

The copy of the entries on the register was a photocopy, known as an office
copy, obtained from the Land Registry. At the bottom of each sheet it
said: 'Issued by the Tunbridge Wells District Land Registry showing the
subsisting entries on the Register on 21 May 1974'. The part of the register
which set out the restrictive covenants had already been sent to Matthew
with the draft contract. He now received the rest.

The purpose of sending a copy of the entries on the register was to prove
that Mr Timms really was the owner of 14 Twintree Avenue, Minford, and
that he was in a position to transfer that property to Matthew, without any
snags or liabilities, as he had undertaken by contract to do.

At the top of the register was the title number: SY 43271604, as in the
contract. Immediately below was part A, the property register, containing
a description of the property:

COUNTY OR COUNTY BOROUGH   PARISH OR PLACE
SURREY   MINFORD

The Freehold land shown and edged with red on the plan of the above
Title filed at the Registry, registered on 19 January 1960 being land and
building on the east side of Twintree Avenue. Property now known as
14 Twintree Avenue.

The proprietorship register, part B of the register, was equally uncomplicated and easy to understand. 'Title Absolute' it said at the top. This was important, as it was with title absolute that Mr Timms had undertaken, in the contract, to sell the house. 'Possessory Title' would by no means have been accetable there. Underneath was the name of the present registered proprietor of the property: 'WILLIAM HERBERT TIMMS of 14 Twintree Avenue, Minford, Surrey, Electrical Engineer, registered on 17 November 1965.' As this was the person who had agreed to sell the property to Matthew, all was well. If the buyer should find that the name on the register is not that of the seller, it would be necessary for him to have legal assistance. The property register also disclosed that Mr Timms had paid £5700 for the house when he bought it in 1965.

The charges register, part C of the register, contained two entries. The first read as follows;

'17 June 1960—A Transfer dated 14 June 1960 by Minford Estates Developments Limited (Vendor) to Bernard Simon Isaacs (Purchaser) contains restrictive covenants. A copy of the covenants is set out in the Schedule of Restrictive Covenants annexed hereto.'

This was something which Matthew had already been into. Right at the start of the transaction he had received, with Dodds & Son's letter dated 23 May, a copy of the schedule of restrictive covenants, which set them out in full. His only concern at this stage was making sure that there were no other restrictive covenants affecting the property, any, that is, of which he had not been informed before exchange of contracts. There were none, so all was well in that respect.

The other entry in the charges register related to Mr Timms's existing mortgage:

17 November 1965—CHARGE dated 10 November 1965 registered on 17 November 1965 to secure the moneys therein mentioned.

PROPRIETOR—MINFORD BUILDING SOCIETY of 102 Great Winchester Street, Minford, Surrey, registered on 17 November 1965.

This showed that Mr Timms had borrowed money from the Minford Building Society and that they had a mortgage on the property. The 'proprietor' referred to in the charges register meant the proprietor of the mortgage, the building society which had lent the money, as distinct from the proprietor of the registered land itself, the one whose name appeared in the proprietorship register, who was Mr Timms.

The payment of what Mr Timms owed the Minford Building Soceity, so that his mortgage would effectively be paid off, would have to be made when Matthew's purchase was being completed. Matthew had to make sure that the Minford Building Society would not have any right to claim that the house was still mortgaged to them once it had become his property. He could not risk being in a position where he might be forced to pay part of what was Mr Timms's debt to the Minford Building Society. This, although quite usual, was the one adverse entry on the register. Matthew would require Dodds & Son to remedy the matter at completion.

REQUISITIONS ON TITLE: BUYER TO SELLER

Matthew was now in a position to prepare his requisitions on title. These are supplementary questions about the property. There is a printed form commonly used for this, one of those which Matthew had obtained from Oyez Publishing Ltd., and was headed: 'REQUISITIONS ON TITLE'. It was form Con. 28B, and was specifically for use where most of the information which a buyer needs to have about a property has already been provided in answer to the enquiries before contract.

Certain of the printed questions on the form were inappropriate for the purchase of 14 Twintree Avenue. Question 2(B) (dealing with the rent and insurance), question 7 (dealing with notification about the sale of the property), were appropriate for the sale of a leasehold property and would only be asked in the purchase of a leasehold house. This was a freehold property, so Matthew crossed them out. He also crossed out question 3, part of which only applied to unregistered land, and the other part (which did apply to registered land) only had to be asked where no office copy of the entries on the register has been supplied and where the land certificate was on deposit at the land registry, which only happens as a rule where one property is being sold off from an estate or block of properties. This left only question 1, which asked for confirmation that the answers given to the enquiries before contract a week or so before were still valid, question 2(A), which asked for receipts for rates and other outgoings to be produced and arrears allowed for, question 4, dealing with the existing mortgage, requiring that it should be paid off at completion. Question 5 asked where completion would take place, or if it could be by post, and about payment. Question 6 stated that vacant possession must be given on completion.

Question 4 referred to mortgages and required that proof would have to be given that Mr Timms's mortgage had been paid off, and asked how this would be done. Where the title is registered, it is common for a Land Registry form (53) to be used by the building society for discharging an existing mortgage. For some strange reason, building societies (and other lenders) often find it difficult to arrange for form 53 to be ready at completion, and instead hand over a solicitor's undertaking to provide it within so-many days. The question asked whether form 53 would be used on completion or if an undertaking was to be used, what it would say.

The form of requisitions on title, like the enquiries before contract, had a bit of space for additional questions to be written in, applicable to the particular sale in question; Matthew added one:

'Please supply an additional authority to inspect the register, addressed to Hodgson, Green & Co. of 67 Lomax Street, Minford, who act for my intended mortgagees.'

The necessity for adding this arose from what Hodgson, Green & Co. had said in the second paragraph of their letter to Matthew of 12 June. Among the items they had asked to receive was an 'authority for us to inspect the register'. This implied that, although Matthew would be making his official search on form 94A just before completion, Hodgson, Green & Co. wanted to make one too, on behalf of the Forthright Building Society. For this they would need an authority from the solicitors for the existing registered owner, Mr Timms, and it was for this extra authority, on top of the authority Matthew had already received for his own use, that he was presently asking in his requisitions on title.

The form of requisitions on title was now ready to be signed and sent to Dodds & Son. Matthew sent off an extra copy of his requisitions on title, so that Dodds and Son could retain one copy for their file and send the other back to him with their replies in the spaces provided.

TRANSFER

Matthew also now prepared the form of the transfer, the document—or, to be exact, the deed, for it would require to be signed, sealed and delivered—which would transfer the ownership of the house from Mr Timms to himself. He wrote:

38 Broastone Drive,
Hastings, Sussex.
26 June 1974.

Dear Sirs,

14 Twintree Avenue, Minford

Thank you for your letter of 24 June and enclosures.

I now send a few requisitions on title, and subject to satisfactory replies thereto, draft transfer with a copy for your use. If the draft is approved, please treat the top copy as the engrossment.

Yours faithfully,
M. J. Seaton

Messrs. Dodds & Son

it was easy to fill in the forms

The transfer is the most important part of the whole transaction. Yet of all the forms that had to be filled in, this was the easiest. Form 19 was the one for use where the title number of the property covers just the one property, that is the one being sold, so that the whole of the registered property has to be transferred. Hence this form is headed: 'Transfer of Whole'. A different form would have to be used where only part of the registered property, one house out of ten, say, was being transferred.

Matthew prepared the transfer thus:

TRANSFER OF WHOLE (Freehold or Leasehold)

County
and district   } Surrey
(or London borough)
    Title Number—SY 43271604

Property—14 Twintree Avenue, Minford
Date ....
In consideration of sixteen thousand two hundred and fifty pounds
(£16250) the receipt whereof is hereby acknowledged

   I, WILLIAM HERBERT TIMMS
     of 14 Twintree Avenue,
      Minford, Surrey,
      Electrical Engineer

                 as beneficial owner hereby transfer to:

   MATTHEW JOHN SEATON
     of 38 Broadstone Drive,
      Hastings, Sussex,
      School teacher
the land comprised in the title above mentioned.

It is hereby certified that the transaction hereby effected does not form
part of a larger transaction or series of transactions in respect of which the
amount or value of aggregate amount or value of the consideration exceeds
£20000.

Signed, sealed and delivered by the said William
Herbert Timms in the presence of:

Name..
Address..   } .... Seal
       ....
Occupation ....

There was a space at the top, left blank for the time being. After completion, the Inland Revenue would emboss the appropriate stamps when the stamp duty had been paid. Also left blank for the time being were the date (the completion date would be filled in there eventually) and, of course, the space where Mr Timms would sign.

With the copy of the entries on the register in front of him, it was easy for Matthew to fill in the form of the transfer with the name of the county or the borough and the short description of the property, as well as the all-important title number. Mr Timms's full name and address were as shown in the proprietorship register. If his present address had been different from his address as shown in the proprietorship register, Matthew would have had to say: 'formerly of .... but now of 14 Twintree Avenue, Minford, Surrey' to make the transfer tally with the register.

As Mr Timms was the actual owner as well as being the person in whom the legal title was vested, he was selling as beneficial owner (as stated in the contract) and not in any other capacity. Hence the words 'beneficial owner' appeared in the transfer.

Matthew and his wife Emma had considered whether to put the house into their joint names. A primary reason for doing so used to be a likely saving in estate duty. Estate duty has now been replaced by capital transfer tax and does not have to be paid on what a husband leaves to his wife, or vice versa.

Where a husband and wife buy a house jointly they should agree between them what is to happen when one of them dies: will the property then automatically go to the survivor, or will the dead partner's share in the house comprise part of his or her estate? Where the property is to pass automatically to the survivor of two people who own a property jointly, they are said to be joint tenants. There will then be no need to enquire into the will of the dead joint tenant: the surviving joint tenant has full power to deal with the property in every way, including power to sell the property, and can give a valid receipt for the money. Where the property is held so that, when one dies, his share passes under his will, and not necessarily directly to the surviving partner, this is called a tenancy in common (the survivor cannot give a valid receipt).

Where the title is registered, the complications involved in joint ownership are few. In the transfer (form 19 JP), the names of both buyers are included. No indication has to be given whether they are holding the property as joint tenants or tenants in common. In the Seatons' case the transfer would have said that Mr Timms transferred the property to:

"Matthew John Seaton, school teacher, and Emma Caroline Seaton, his wife, both of 38 Broadstone Drive, Hastings, Sussex". In the Seatons' actual case the house was to be in Matthew's name alone.

There is space on the back of form 19 for any special clauses that may have to be added, should this be necessary. In the case of 14 Twintree Avenue there were none. The only other item that had to be added was the figure at the end of the certificate of value, the final sentence at the end of the transfer which is there because of stamp duty. Where the price is £15000 or less, the stamp duty payable is nil; from £15001 to £20000 the rate of stamp duty is one half per cent; between £20001 and £25000, the rate is one per cent; between £25001 and £30000, the rate is 1½ per cent; over £30001 the rate is 2 per cent. The Inland Revenue is alive to the wiles of taxpayers and foresaw that, unless something was done about it, many people buying a house for, say, £15400, for which the stamp duty is £77, would transfer part of the house for perhaps £10000 and pay no stamp duty on it as the price was under £15000; and the other part by a separate transfer for £5400, and again pay no stamp duty for the same reason. The same device could be used with a purchase at a price above £20000 or £25000 to avoid paying the higher rate that applies above those figures. In order, therefore, to make it possible for no duty at all to be paid if the price does not exceed £15000, and pay the reduced rates of duty to be paid on prices from between £15001 and £30000, a certificate of value in the words stated has to be included in the transfer. The figure of £15000 goes in the certificate where the price is less than that; if it is from £15001 to £20000, the figure of £20000 goes in. For cases between £20001 and £25000, the figure of £25000 is included, and for cases between £25001 and £30000, the figure to use is £30000. If the price is more than that, the certificate of value can be crossed out on the printed form. The stamp duty is at the rate of two per cent of the purchase price then, anyway.

Lawyers tend to prepare a document in draft and submit the draft to the solicitor acting for the other person involved. So simple is the form of 'TRANSFER OF WHOLE' that there is not much room for argument about how it should be worded, so that the stage of submitting the deed in draft is often dispensed with.

Matthew prepared four copies of the transfer. Two of them, including the top copy, which was to be used as the engrossment, he sent to Dodds & Son. One copy he kept for his own file. The fourth copy he would shortly be sending to Hodgson, Green & Co., acting for his building society.

Dodds & Son replied to Matthew's letter of 26 June:

Dodds & Son   *1, Charter Street,*
   Solicitors   *Minford, Surrey.*
                                                     28th June, 1974.
Dear Sir,
                     14 Twintree Avenue, Minford
   We now return your Requisitions on Title, together with our replies. We approve the form of the draft Transfer, and, in accordance with your suggestion, are treating the top copy as the engrossment, and shall have this executed by our client. We are obliged to you for the spare copies of the requisitions and of the Transfer which you have sent for our file.
   We shall be in touch with you again nearer completion date.
                         Yours faithully,
                         Dodds & Son
M. J. Seaton, Esq.

Sometimes a seller's solicitor adds a clause to the transfer to the effect that the buyer will comply with the restrictive covenants, and will indemnify the seller for any future liability that might arise from a breach of the covenants. There is no reason why the buyer should not agree to this. However, few solicitors feel it necessary to add this clause; Dodds & Son did not, and approved the transfer as drawn by Matthew.

Dodds & Son's answers to Matthew's requisitions on title were adequate. They confirmed that their answers to the enquiries before contract still stood, and that suitable evidence about the payment of rates and other outgoings would be produced at completion. They said that the existing mortgage with the Minford Building Society would 'of course' be paid off at completion and added that they would give an unqualified undertaking, if form 53 could not be handed over at completion. This meant that if the building society holding Mr Timms's mortgage could not provide the official form saying the mortgage was paid off, they—Dodds & Son, or the solicitors for the building society—would give a personal and unqualified undertaking to see that the form came without 14 days. They said that they would defer till later saying where completion would take place and how and to whom the money should be paid. They confirmed that vacant possession of the property would be given on completion. Finally, Dodds & Son sent an additional authority to inspect the register, so that Hodgson, Green & Co., as well as Matthew, would be able to make a search on form 94A at the Land Registry just before completion.

BUILDING SOCIETY'S SOLICITORS
Matthew was now ready to start dealing with Hodgson, Green & Co., the solicitors acting for the Forthright Building Society, which would be lending him most of the purchase price. He wrote this letter to them:

> *38 Broadstone Drive,*
> *Hastings, Sussex.*
> *30 June 1974.*

Dears Sirs,
> *14 Twintree Avenue, Minford*
> *I duly received, and now thank you for, your letter of 12 June 1974.*
> *I now enclose the following:*
> *1—contract dated 24 June 1974;*
> *2—enquiries before contract and replies;*
> *3—local search and enquiries with replies;*
> *4—office copy entries on the register, and plan;*
> *5—requisitions on title and replies;*
> *6—draft transfer as approved by the seller's solicitors;*
> *7—authority for you to inspect the register.*
> *I shall be glad to know what further requirements, if any, you have in this matter and to receive the draft mortgage deed for approval.*
> *Yours faithfully,*
> *M. J. Seaton*

Messrs. Hodgson, Green & Co.

He was about to part with some of the most important documents concerning his purchase and would probably never see them again, because a building society usually keeps all the documents. He therefore had photocopies made of the contract, the enquiries before contract and replies, the local search and enquiries with replies, office copy entries on the register and plans, and the requisitions on titles and replies.

If he had not been able to take photocopies, he would have made a note on the inside cover of his files of the date when the office copy of the entries on the register was issued from the Land Registry. A note at the bottom of each page of the copy entries on the register stated that the copy showed 'the subsisting entries on the register on 24 MAY 1974'; that was the date on which the copy was issued. Matthew would need to know that date when he came to fill in his application for an official search of the register on form 94A, which he would be doing in a few weeks' time, just before completion.

It was a week before he had a reply:

Hodgson, Green & Co.   *67, Lomax Street,*
Solicitors   *Minford, Surrey.*
                                                                        5th July, 1974.
Dear Sir,
                          14 Twintree Avenue, Minford
We duly received your letter of 30th ult. and enclosures.
We enclose a few requisitions on title for your attention. We also enclose a draft
mortgage for your approval. As you will see the mortgage deed is in a standard form
and our clients do not permit variations from it.
Upon hearing from you upon these matters we shall be sending you the engrossment
mortgage deed for execution.
                                   Yours faithfully,
                           Hodgson, Green & Co.
M. J. Seaton, Esq.

Here, then, were another lot of questions, requisitions on title, this time addressed to Matthew. A buyer's building society had no direct relationship with a seller, and so although some of the answers may be coming from the seller, the questions are put to the buyer. Sometimes, instead of sending off requisitions on title to the seller's solicitor earlier on, the buyer waits until he has received from the building society's solicitors their requisitions on title. He combines the building society's requisitions with any he himself wants to ask into one complete set of requisitions, and answers the building society's requisitions by using the information he has obtained from the seller's solicitor. Matthew had not adopted this procedure.

There is no one standard form in common use by building societies for these requisitions. Different solicitors use different forms; sometimes they are printed or duplicated. It may also happen that no requisitions as such are asked at all, if the title is registered; any points which need to be dealt with are then raised in a letter.

Hodgson, Green & Co. in this case framed their own questions. The layout for this form looked pretty much the same as the layout of the forms of enquiries before contract (Conveyancing 29 Long), and the buyer's requisitions on title (form Con. 28B). All three had in common that the questions were set out in the left-hand column and a space for the answers was provided alongside the questions in the right-hand column. The questions asked, and the answers Matthew gave, were as follows:

REQUISITIONS ON TITLE
SEATON—and FORTHRIGHT BUILDING SOCIETY
14 TWINTREE AVENUE, MINFORD

1. Please confirm that the borrower is finding the full amount of the purchase price, apart from this mortgage loan, out of his own funds.

   1. *I so confirm*

2. We shall require to receive on completion the following:
   (1) Charge Certificate;
   (2) Form 53 duly executed or an undertaking;
   (3) Transfer duly executed by vendor;
   (4) Land Registry form A4 duly completed;
   (5) LVA form duly completed;
   (6) Mortgage Deed duly executed in the presence of a solicitor;
   (7) Search certificate (94A) not more than 20 days old

   2. *Noted; with regard to (6), as you know I am not represented by a solicitor. Would it suffice if I were to execute the mortgage deed at completion, in the presence of your representative attending completion? If not, what do you suggest?*

3. Please confirm that the borrower intends to move into full possession at completion and that no lettings of any kind are contemplated.

   3. *I so confirm*

4. Where will completion take place?

   4. *I am enquiring.*

Dated 5th July, 1974

Dated 7 July 1974

Hodgson, Green & Co.
Proposed mortgagees' solicitors

M. J. Seaton
borrower

Building societies often like to know that a buyer is providing the whole of the rest of the money himself, that is, the difference between the price and the amount being borrowed. They feel happier if the borrower has a significant stake of his own in the property, as they feel that he would therefore be less likely to default on the mortgage. If he is borrowing from elsewhere, they like to know this. Matthew was not, and said so in reply to the first question.

The list of documents which Hodgson, Green & Co. would require at completion was set out at this stage, so as to prevent any misunderstanding later. To make sure nothing is forgotten, the building society's solicitor specifies in advance exactly what he expects to get.

One small problem did present itself at this point. The Forthright Building Society required, apparently, that a borrower should sign, seal and deliver the mortgage deed in the presence of a solicitor, so that the solicitor would sign it as the witness. This is quite a common requirement. Where a borrower is legally represented, his own solicitor is usually the witness to the borrower's execution of the mortgage deed. He executes it usually some time before completion, although the mortgage does not become operative until then. In this case, because Matthew was not represented, he suggested that he should execute the deed when he personally attended for completion, as he would then be able to execute it in the presence of whoever from Hodgson Green & Co. attended completion. Alternatively, of course, they might, if asked, have waived this. There is no requirement in law that the deed must be witnessed by a solicitor.

Question 3 of these requisitions merely required written confirmation from Matthew that only he and his family would be occupying the house. Building societies are understandably nervous about the possibility of a house being let, and of their being landed, maybe, with tenants without being able to get rid of them. A house with tenants living in it, especially if they are protected tenants, is worth less than the same house when vacant, as a rule. Furthermore, a buyer sometimes plans to let part of a house, with the idea that the rent should help him with the mortgage payments, and he may try to conceal this plan from the building society so as not to jeopardise the loan. A formal confirmation on this point is therefore frequently sought in the building society's requisitions on title.

Finally, the requisitions asked where completion would be taking place. Matthew was not sure at the moment. The general rule is that completion takes place at the office of the solicitor acting for the seller's building society, or often by post. Matthew knew, from the entries on the charges register, that Mr Timms had a mortgage with the Minford Building Society, which would be paid off at completion. He assumed, therefore, that completion would take place at the office of the solicitors acting for the Minford Building Society. He did not yet know who they were. Had it not been for the fact that Mr Timms had an existing mortgage, completion would be taking place at the office of his solicitors, Dodds & Son. The undertaking about form 53—if one was to be provided—would come from the Minford Building Society's solicitors and would provide that the form should be made available to Hodgson, Green & Co. within 14 days of completion.

THE MORTGAGE DEED

Hodgson, Green & Co.'s letter of 5 July had also enclosed the draft mortgage deed. It was a printed document, with some blank spaces in it, mainly at the beginning and the end, which had been filled in with details special to the transaction.

Matthew carefully checked these, to see that his name was spelt correctly, that the house was correctly described and that the title number was accurately stated. Matthew was not surprised to find an embargo on amendments to the draft mortgage deed. This often happens. Sometimes a building society's solicitor sends the draft mortgage with a copy, the idea being that one should be retained and the other sent back approved, following normal conveyancing procedure for the approval of draft documents. In other cases, as here, the building society's solicitor sends one copy only of the draft mortgage deed, because, from a practical point of view, there is no question of approving the draft mortgage; it is a case of take it or leave it. In yet other cases, the building society's solicitor sends straightaway the engrossment of the mortgage deed, usually with a copy, without going through the formality of sending a draft first. The practice varies, depending on the building society. Insurance companies, local authorities and others who lend money on mortgage also vary in what they do in this respect.

Matthew approved the draft mortgage as it stood, and was not perturbed by the fact that the Forthright Building Society 'do not permit variations'. The deed was lengthy, running to several closely printed pages. It set out many things including what the building society could do, such as selling the property, if he did not make the promised payments under the mortgage.

Much of it was rather incomprehensible to him. Many lawyers, if asked what the exact effect was of some of the clauses in a mortgage deed, would have to look up the answer in a text-book. Of all the legal documents that are commonly found, the mortgage deed takes the prize for prolixity and incomprehensibility. The deed may be described as a 'mortgage' or as a 'legal charge'. In practice, it makes no difference.

There was one clause in the mortgage which Matthew did hunt for, and find. That was the one which dealt with the notice the building society required if and when he wished to pay off the mortgage in a lump sum. Mortgages vary in this respect; some require three months' notice, some require longer, some shorter. It means this: when an owner is selling his house and so able—and indeed obliged—to repay his mortgage, he should, as soon as a binding contract to sell has been signed, notify the building society of his intention to pay off the mortgage loan. He will then have to pay interest on the mortgage up to a day three months (or however long the period of notice is) later. This is so, even though the money may be actually repaid earlier, after, say, only four weeks.

The mortgage deed also dealt with several of the matters which were referred to in the notification of 5 June that Matthew had received from the Forthright Building Society. There was a clause which enabled the society, on giving three months' notice, to alter the rate of interest. There was another clause which, by excluding the borrower's rights under section 99 of the Law of Property Act 1925, forbade Matthew to let the house, 'or any part thereof'. There was also a clause which required him to insure the property 'with a company to be approved by the society', and the amount of the insurance was to be in 'a sum not less than the full value thereof for the time being'.

Matthew now replied to Hodgson, Green & Co.:

38 Broadstone Drive,
Hastings, Sussex.
7 July 1974.

Dear Sirs,

14 Twintree Avenue, Minford

Thank you for you letter of 5 July. I now return your requisitions with my answers. I confirm that the draft mortgage is approved as drawn, and I am retaining if for my file. I look forward to hearing from you with the engrossment.

I will be grateful if you will let me know as soon as possible the amount that will be available on completion, after deducting all expenses.

Yours faithfully,
M. J. Seaton

Messrs. Hodgson, Green & Co.

He put the draft mortgage deed in his file. Ultimately this draft would constitute his copy of the mortgage, the copy he would permanently keep, for although he would shortly receive the engrossment of the mortgage deed for execution by him, that engrossment would, after completion, be the mortgage deed itself and would therefore be retained by the building society. He would obviously need to keep a copy of the elaborate clauses to which he would be putting his name.

Matthew needed to know precisely what deductions the Forthright Building Society would be making from the loan of £13000. That is why he asked for these details when he wrote to Hodgson, Green & Co.

He would also need to know exactly how much money would have to be paid to Mr Timms on completion day: would it be the price less deposit (£14625, in fact), or would the rates and water rates be apportioned, to make it a slightly different figure? To find out, he wrote to Dodds & Son:

> *38 Broadstone Drive,*
> *Hastings, Sussex.*
> *7 July 1974.*

Dear Sirs,
> *14 Twintree Avenue, Minford*
> *I refer to your letter of 28 June, and I shall be obliged if you will let me have a completion statement made up to 26 July, as soon as possible. Presumably you will require the sum to be paid in the form of a banker's draft.*
> *Please arrange for the keys to be handed over at completion, or, if more convenient, to be left with the agents.*
> *Can you now let me know where completion will take place?*
> > *Yours faithfully*
> > *M. J. Seaton*

Messrs. Dodds & Son.

A banker's draft is a cheque signed by the bank manager (or one of his staff), so there can be no doubt that it will be met when presented for payment. It is the accepted and usual practice between solicitors to carry out the financial side of the transfer of property by banker's draft; it is by banker's draft that a seller's solicitor usually requires to receive the purchase money at completion, and it is by banker's draft that a seller's building society usually requires to be paid the necessary amount to pay off the existing mortgage.

Matthew now heard from Hodgson, Green & Co.:

Hodgson, Green & Co.   *67 Lomax Street,*
> *Solicitors*   *Minford, Surrey.*
> *12th July, 1974.*

Dear Sir,
> *14 Twintree Avenue, Minford*
> *We thank you for your letter of the 7th inst.*
> *With regard to your query on our requisition 2(6), it will be quite in order if you execute the mortgage deed (the engrossment of which we now enclose) at completion in the presence of the writer. This, of course, is on the assumption that completion takes place in this town. If it does not, it would be necessary for you to make some alternative arrangement about executing the mortgage. We enclose also a copy of the Society's rules for your retention.*
> *We enclose a statement showing £12765.43 as being available on completion, after*

deducting the expenses shown. If it is required that this sum be provided in split
drafts, please let us know as soon as possible, and in any event not later than 3 days
before completion, the amount of each draft and to whom it should be payable.

Yours faithfully,
Hodgson, Green & Co.

M. J. Seaton, Esq.

This solved the problem of the requirement that the mortgage deed
should be executed in the presence of a solicitor. Hodgson, Green & Co.
did not yet know whether completion would take place in Minford or not;
neither, indeed, did Matthew. Often a solicitor, acting in a transaction to
be completed at some distance from his office, instructs another solicitor,
who practises in the locality where completion will take place, to act as his
agent for the purpose. In their letter, Hodgson, Green & Co. suggested
that if that happened, some alternative arrangement would have to be
made regarding Matthew's execution of the mortgage deed. This might
entail having another of the solicitors there to witness the execution of the
deed by Matthew. Any solicitor can be asked to witness a signature for a
small fee (£1). In the event, the point did not arise, as completion took
place in Minford after all.

Matthew checked that the engrossment of the mortgage deed was in
accordance with the draft which he had approved. He left it unsigned and
undated; signing and dating would be done at completion.

Hodgons, Green & Co. enclosed a copy of the rules of the Forthright
Building Society for Matthew to keep. He had had to become a member
of the society in order to obtain a mortgage, and as a member he was
entitled to a copy of the rules. In most cases a potential borrower must
become a member of the society that will lend him the money, but such
membership is little more than a formality. Matthew found it difficult to
summon the energy to read the rules at this juncture, but he did.

Rather more important for the moment was the statement which Hodgson, Green & Co. sent with their letter, showing how much of the loan
would be left after the expenses had been deducted:

SEATON and FORTHRIGHT BUILDING SOCIETY
re: 14 TWINTREE AVENUE, MINFORD, SURREY

	£	£
Mortgage advance		13000·00
Deductions:		
(1) Stamp duty on transfer at £16250	81·25	
(2) Land Registry fees	42·50	
(3) Our costs (including VAT)	88·32	
(4) Insurance premium	22·50	
		less 234·57
Net sum available at completion		12765·43

These expenses, which were to be deducted from the loan, were Matthew's main expenses of the whole transaction. Hodgson, Green & Co. were going to deduct them from the loan because they would be taking away with them after completion the transfer deed, the mortgage deed and the other documents, and accordingly it was they, and not Matthew, who would be physically paying the stamp duty to the Inland Revenue when they took the transfer to be stamped. But it was Matthew's responsibility, as buyer, to bear the cost. Accordingly, the amount of the stamp duty was to be deducted from the loan. The same applied to the Land Registry fees; after stamping the deeds, Hodgson, Green & Co. would be sending them to the Land Registry with the charge certificate. At the same time they would have to send the Land Registry fees, and since these fees were also Matthew's liability, these too had to be deducted from the loan.

Hodgson, Green & Co.'s legal costs also fell into much the same category. They naturally wished to be sure that they would be paid, and—as made clear to Matthew right from the start—he would have to pay them. So they deducted their fees, too. Finally, the insurance premium was deducted also. The house was already covered with the Bridstow Insurance Company, and had been since exchange of contracts. The building society, to make sure that the first premium did not go unpaid, deducted the amount, and paid it direct to the insurance company.

Matthew checked the figures for each of these deductions; each one was correct. The stamp duty on the transfer, £81·25, was at the rate of one half per cent on the price of £16250. The Land Registry fees were on the scale

D

laid down, and were also calculated on the price of £16250. They came to £42·50. There is no extra Land Registry fee to pay for the mortgage.

There is a scale of fees to be paid to a solicitor who deals with the legal side of a building society mortgage where the mortgage is for not more than £25000. This scale has been agreed between the Law Society (the governing body of solicitors) and the Building Societies Association, to which most building societies belong. Where a solicitor acts only for the building society he charges a fee on this scale. If the borrower has a solicitor acting for him and a different solicitor is acting for the building society, each may charge a fee on this scale for dealing with the mortgage (the borrower's own solicitor may reduce the fee). In Matthew's case, the mortgage was for less than £25000, so the scale applied and they charged £76·80 plus VAT. Above £25000, the scale is not binding, and solicitors can charge whatever is fair and reasonable.

The last item in the statement sent by Hodgson, Green & Co. was for the insurance premium. The Building Society arranged with the Bridstow Insurance Company that the amount of the insurance cover should be equal to the full value of the property. Matthew remembered that the price that he was paying was not necessarily the amount in which the insurance ought to be: a property needs to be insured to cover the whole cost of rebuilding it, should it be totally destroyed. Seeing that the land was already there, so to speak, the cost of rebuilding could possibly be less than the present value of the property—which Matthew was content to assume was the same as the price he was paying, £16250. But, on the other hand, it might well cost more to rebuild it than the amount of the present value, especially if the cost of everything involved, such as the architect's fee and clearing the site of the ruins of the house, were included. It is therefore wise to insure a house for a sum which represents a fair estimate of the total cost of rebuilding in the event of its being completely destroyed. Matthew had reckoned that this was £18000, and it was for this amount that the Forthright Building Society had arranged the insurance for Twin-tree Avenue. The Bridstow Insurance Company charged an annual premium at the rate of 12½p for every £100 of the amount insured for their comprehensive insurance on a house. On £18000 this was £22·50, and this was the amount correctly charged for this item on the statement sent by the building society's solicitors.

Thus the statement sent by Hodgson, Green & Co. showing that a total of £234·57 would be deducted from the loan at completion was correct, leaving a net sum of £12765·43 available.

COMPLETION STATEMENT
Three days later Matthew heard from Dodds & Sons:

Dodds & Son   *1 Charter Street,*
  Solicitors   *Minford, Surrey.*
                                                                 15th July, 1974.
Dear Sir,
                    14 Twintree Avenue, Minford
We now enclose completion statement made up to the 26th July.
Completion will take place at the offices of Messrs. Anderson, James & Pringle,
88 Great Winchester Street, Minford, solicitors for the existing mortgagees. We
confirm that the balance required to complete must be paid by banker's draft or in
cash and split as indicated in the note on the completion statement.
We have noted what you say about the keys.
                              Yours faithfully,
                              Dodds & Son
M. J. Seaton, Esq.

The completion statement enclosed with this letter showed the amount
of money which Dodds & Son calculated was due to Mr Timms at completion. It looked like this:

TIMMS TO SEATON
14 Twintree Avenue, Minford, Surrey

COMPLETION STATEMENT
made up to 26 July 1974

		£
Purchase price		16250
Less deposit		1625
		14625
Add:		
Proportion of general rates from 26 July to 30 September 1974 (66 days) at £225 per annum	40·68	
Proportion of water rates for same period (66 days) at £16·20 per annum	2·92	43·60
		£14668·60

N.B. 1. Please produce deposit release at completion.
  2. Please provide the above sum in two drafts in favour of:
      (i) Minford Building Society for   £3738·07
      (ii) Ourselves (Dodds & Son) for   £10930·53
                                                                              ——————
                                                                              £14668·60
                                                                              ——————

Matthew checked the items in the completion statement. The price, £16250, less the deposit £1625, was right. Then, to the balance of £14625 something was added on account of rates and water rates. If the seller has not yet paid the current rates (in April or October, say) a proportion of them is deducted, not added. The hypothesis here was that Mr Timms had already paid the rates and water rates for the half-year beginning 1 April 1974; £112·50 for the rates to Minford DC, and £8·10 for water rates to the local water authority. But Matthew would be responsible for the proportion of the rates for the period from 26 July to 30 September, when he would be living in the house. This adjustment in liability was made by adding the proportion of the rates and the water rate for this period to the price Matthew had to pay, and that is exactly what the completion statement did. Matthew checked the figures, and agreed that the amount that ought to be added in the completion statement was £43·60. However, he would still have to make sure that the receipts for rates and water rates (or other evidence of their payment, such as a letter from the local or water authority), when inspected by him at completion, showed that the amounts paid were £112·50 and £8·10 respectively. Subject to that, he was satisfied that what was due to be paid to Mr Timms would be £14668·60.

There is, in fact, no need for rates to be apportioned. It is perfectly easy to arrange that the seller and the buyer should each pay his appropriate proportion direct to the local council. If the seller has already paid the rates in advance, he will get a refund, and the buyer will in due course get a demand for the sum due from him. A letter to the local authority explaining the change of ownership, giving the date, is all that is needed.

In the case of leasehold property, the ground rent payable to the landlord and the annual insurance premium have also to be apportioned. Ground rent is usually paid in arrears on each quarter day, or half-yearly. This ground rent is generally paid to the landlord without deducting income tax. It used to be the rule that tax was deducted at the standard rate, but this is no longer so, except where the landlord lives abroad. Generally, the insurance premium has to be apportioned because the buyer has no option but to take over the existing policy, if the lease so requires. The apportionment of the insurance premium is made to date from exchange of contracts, the day when the property started to be at the buyer's risk.

All that has to be done in order to apportion liability for gas and electricity between the seller and the buyer is for the seller to arrange to have the meters read on the day he gives possession to the buyer. Separate bills will then be sent to the seller and buyer by the electricity board and gas region. If the telephone is being taken over, the rental should also be apportioned.

There were two notes at the bottom of the completion statement Dodds & Son has sent. One asked for a deposit release. Matthew would have to provide this at completion. It would be a letter addressed to Flint & Morgan allowing them to hand over to Mr Timms the deposit of £100, which they were holding as stakeholders. The other note dealt with the way in which the £14668·60 would be required to be split when it came to completion. Matthew had known from the time when he first received a copy of the charges register that Mr Timms still had a mortgage with the Minford Building Society; Dodds & Son had confirmed that this mortgage would be paid off at completion. It came as no surprise, therefore, to find that it would be necessary to split the amount required to complete— £14668·60—into two parts. Dodds & Son had apparently been told by the Minford Building Society that the amount required to pay off Mr Timms's mortgage on 26 July would be £3738·07. To bring about the necessary repayment of this mortgage at completion, therefore, Matthew had to pay part of the balance of the price in the form of a banker's draft for £3738·07 in favour of the Minford Building Society. The remaining £10930·53 would be paid to Dodds & Son, to be passed on to Mr Timms himself. It can happen that completion monies have to be split three or even four ways, instead of just two as here. If Mr Timms was to have been completing the purchase of another house on the same day on which he was to complete his sale of 14 Twintree Avenue, then some splitting of bank drafts might have been necessary on that purchase as well. If that had happened, then Matthew might have found that the £10930·53 would have had to be split again: part, maybe, to some distant building society with a mortgage on the house Mr Timms was buying, and the rest to the solicitors for the person selling that house. That completion did not arise here. Matthew now had all the figures he needed in order to make the final financial calculations for completion.

It was not just the legal side of his purchase which was taking Matthew's time, of course. There was much activity elsewhere: clearing out, packing up, arranging for the removal men, arranging about telephones and to have the meters read, getting change of address cards prepared and sent off (including one to 'Which?') deciding what was to go where, and all the other rigmarole of moving, quite apart from everything involved in disposing of his present house.

He learnt on the phone from Mr Timms that he had arranged to move out of 14 Twintree Avenue on 25 July so that the house would be ready for the Seatons on 26 July, the day fixed by the contract for completion. Unless a special arrangement is made, the seller does not let the buyer take possession until completion has actually taken place and the money has been handed over. There might be a last-minute hitch, which could conceivably result in the sale never being completed, in which case things might be very awkward for the seller if the buyer had already moved in.

Having therefore made firm arrangements with Mr Timms about moving out and moving in, Matthew wrote to Dodds & Son:

> *38 Broadstone Drive,*
> *Hastings, Sussex.*
> *17 July 1974.*

Dear Sirs,
> *14 Twintree Avenue, Minford*
> *Thank you for your letter of 15 July enclosing the completion statement. I note that the amount required to complete is £14668·60 of which £3738·07 is to go to the Minford Building Society.*
>
> *I understand that your client is moving out on 25 July and that the keys will be handed over by you at completion. Is this right?*
>
> *I shall be moving in during the afternoon of the 26th all being well. An appointment at, say 2 p.m. would suit me for completion. Would you let me know whether this is acceptable to Messrs. Anderson, James & Pringle? The solicitors for my mortgagees, Messrs. Hodgson, Green & Co., are able to fit in with this suggestion.*
> > *Yours faithfully,*
> > *M. J. Seaton*

Messrs. Dodds & Son.

Matthew assumed that he was not to be allowed to move in until after completion was finished, and that the keys to enable him to get in would be handed over at completion first. He hoped to arrange an appointment to complete early in the afternoon of the 26th, so that there would still be sufficient time after completion to move in before the end of the day.

Matthew had phoned Hodgson, Green & Co. about the appointment for completion. He had told them that it would be taking place in Minford at the offices of Anderson, James & Pringle, acting for the Minford Building Society. Two o'clock was a suitable time for Hodgson, Green & Co. Provided, therefore, that Dodds & Son (for Mr Timms) and Anderson, James & Pringle (for the Minford Building Society) could also fit in with the time, it would all work out very nicely. Sometimes there are difficulties in arranging an appointment to meet the convenience of three or four different solicitors.

Matthew wrote to Hodgson, Green & Co., mainly to confirm what he had already told them on the phone:

> *38 Broadstone Drive,*
> *Hastings, Sussex.*
> *17 July 1974.*
>
> *Dear Sirs,*
> *14 Twintree Avenue, Minford*
> *I received your letter of 12 July and note what you say regarding execution of the mortgage deed.*
> *I have now received a completion statement for the seller's solicitors and can tell you how the amount to be made available at completion should be split. Please provide the sum of £12765·43 in two drafts as follows:*
>
> | | |
> |---|---|
> | *(1) in favour of Minford Building Society* | *£3738·07* |
> | *(2) in favour of Dodds & Son* | *£9027·36* |
> | | *————* |
> | | *£12765·43* |
> | | *————* |
>
> *I confirm our telephone conversation to the effect that completion is to take place at the offices of Messrs. Anderson, James & Pringle of 88 Great Winchester Street, Minford on 26 July. The suggested time for completion is 2 pm. I will let you know when and if this time is confirmed.*
> *Yours faithfully,*
> *M. J. Seaton*
> *Messrs. Hodgson, Green & Co.*

Having received a completion statement and having been told how the amount required to be paid at completion should be split. Matthew was able, in this letter to Hodgson, Green & Co., to tell them just how they should split the £12765·43 which they had said they would be able to provide at completion. Dodds & Son had asked for their £14668·60 to be split as follows.

to Minford Building Society	£3738·07
to Dodds & Son	£10930·53
	————
	£14668·60
	————

Consequently, Matthew had worked out that the £12765·43 coming to him from the Forthright Building Society would have to be split into two parts: one for £3738·07, to cover what had to go to the Minford Building Society; and the remaining £9027·36 to help towards meeting Dodds and Son's costs. It was in this way that Matthew came to ask Hodgson, Green and Co. to provide their £12765·43 in the proportions stated in his letter. This would account for only part of the total amount of £14668·60 which Dodds and Son would require to receive. The remaining £1903·17 would be provided out of his own funds.

PREPARING FOR COMPLETION
Matthew now prepared for his own use a memorandum for completion. It looked like this:

---

14 Twintree Avenue: completion 2 p.m. on 26 July 1974 at Anderson, James & Pringle's offices.

Price and costs	£
Price of house	16250·00
Stamp duty on transfer	81·25
Land Registry fees	42·50
Hodgson, Green & Co.'s fees	88·32
Insurance premium	22·50
Building society's valuation fee	37·95
Own survey fee	79·50
Local search fees	5·75
Proportion of rates and water rates	43·60
	£16651·37
less:	£13000·00
	£3651·37

What I actually pay	£
Deposit (10 per cent)	1625·00
Building society's valuation fee	37·95
Own survey fee	79·50
Local search fees	5·75
Dodds & Sons at completion from me	1903·17
	£3651·37

I must take with me to completion: search certificate (form 94A), Land Registry application (form A4), LVA form, mortgage deed, banker's draft payable to Dodds & Son for £1903·17.

Hodgson, Green & Co. (acting for Forthright Building Society) will require from me: search certificate (form 94A), Land Registry application (form A4), LVA form, mortgage deed.

Hodgson, Green & Co. will require from Anderson, James & Pringle (acting for Minford Building Society): charge certificate, form 53 or an undertaking to discharge the existing mortgage; they will require from Dodds & Son (acting for Timms): transfer executed by Timms.

Dodds & Son (acting for Timms) will require from me: banker's draft for £1903·17; they will require from Hodgson, Green & Co.: banker's draft for £9027·36.

Anderson, James & Pringle (acting for Minford Building Society) will require from Hodgson, Green & Co.: banker's draft for £3738·07.

I will require from Dodds & Son: keys, receipts for rates and water rates. (No NHBC certificate because the property is more than ten years old.)

Money (i.e. bankers' drafts)—		
from me		£1903·17
from Forthright B.S.	£3738·07	
from Forthright B.S.	£9027·36	
		£12765·43
due per completion statement		£14668.60
Split thus:		
To: Minford B.S. (from Forthright B.S.)		£3738·07
To: Dodds & Son:		
—from Forthright B.S.	£9027·36	
—from me	£1903·17	
		£10930·53
		£14668·60

This memorandum set out the essence of what was going to happen at completion. It would serve a double purpose: it would be a reminder— Matthew could see himself ticking off the items one by one when the day came, and thus nothing would be overlooked. Secondly, so far as the financial side was concerned, it showed that the calculations made in the completion statement by Dodds & Son and in the statement sent by Hodgson, Green & Co. showing the balance of the mortgage loan, tallied with his own calculations of what the whole transaction would cost him. He was satisfied, once he had prepared his memo, that £1903·17 was the right figure for him to have to provide at completion.

OFFICIAL SEARCH

Matthew had now to make his search at the Land Registry; it is sometimes called an official search. The time factor is important in the case of an official search because it is essential for the buyer to have obtained the search certificate back from the Land Registry before completion actually takes place. He should never complete without it. A building society will not release the money it is lending without a search certificate. The search certificate should be dated as short a time as reasonably practicable before completion. The Land Registry is usually reliable about searches, and an application for an offical search will be sent back within a few days, bearing a search certificate, although it has been known for the registry to take quite a long time under acute pressure. You can phone the district land registry concerned to find out what is the current delay in dealing with searches. The aim is to have a search certificate dated the day before completion, or the day before that. Ideally, solicitors post off the application for the official search about five days before completion, by first class post. The Land Registry certifies it and posts it back two or three days before completion, so that it arrives back before completion.

With completion fixed for 26 July, Matthew reckoned that the day for posting his application for an official search could be 17 July, nine days before. The Registry would then post back the certificate so that he would receive it by 25 July. No weekends intervened, otherwise he would have had to allow for the fact that the registry does not operate on saturdays and sundays.

A search certificate lasts 20 working days only. When issuing a search certificate, the Land Registry is really saying two distinct things. Firstly, it says: 'The register relating to this property has not been changed since the date you mention—that is, the date when we issued a copy of the entries on the register, so that the copy you have is still a true copy.' Secondly, it says: 'If you apply to be registered as owner within 20 working days of today's date, we guarantee that we will not have registered anyone else as the owner in the meantime.' This is a valuable protection to the buyer. There is no other practicable way in which the buyer can be certain that in the short time after the registry has issued the search certificate, but before it has received the buyer's application to be registered as owner, someone else might not slip in and claim to be the owner, as might happen if the seller were trying to operate a fraud on more than one innocent buyer. This is made possible by the 20 day protection given to the person making the search. By getting the search certificate, the buyer makes sure that he has prority for 20 days over anyone else who applies to the registry to be registered as owner or mortgagee. On the 21st day this priority lapses, unless it is extended. If it is not extended, it is essential that the application to register the buyer as owner should reach the registry by 11 a.m. on the twentyfirst working day after the date on which the search certificate was issued (saturdays, sundays and public holidays are excluded in counting up the days). Twenty days are usually quite sufficient.

To give the parties time to manoeuvre, it is best that the search should not be made until about a week before completion takes place. Thus there will still remain, say, 12 working days for stamping the deeds and dealing with any other formalities before the application to register the buyer as owner must reach the registry.

Application for an official search at the Land Registry is made on form 94A. It is a green form, and was one of the forms Matthew had obtained from the Oyez shop. Like the forms on which Matthew had applied for his local search certificates some weeks before, form 94A had a duplicate to be torn off and retained in the Land Registry, the original to be returned to him with the certificate on the back, date-stamped by the registry. Both the original application and the tear-off duplicate had to be filled in by Matthew.

The heart of the form, when completed by Matthew, read in effect as follows: 'I, the above-mentioned applicant, certify that the applicant intends to purchase the whole of the land comprised in the title above-mentioned. The written authority of the registered proprietor (or his solicitors) to inspect the register accompanies this application. Application is made for an official search of the register of the said title to ascertain whether any adverse entry has been made since 21 May 1974, being the date of the issue of an office copy of the existing entries on the register'.

On the back of the form was a list of the offices of the Land Registry. These are Birkenhead, Croydon, Durham, Gloucester, Harrow, Lytham St. Annes, Nottingham, Plymouth, Stevenage, Tunbridge Wells, and Swansea. Each office covers a different area of England and Wales.

To find out which district land registry covers a particular district, phone up any registry (the phone numbers are given on form 94A). In Matthew's case, the search was to go to the Tunbridge Wells registry, as the property was in Surrey. At the bottom of the application form was a space to fill in the name and address to which the search certificate was to be sent. Matthew filled in his own.

In filling in form 94A, Matthew copied the title number from the copy of the draft transfer which he had kept in his file. On the bottom of each sheet of the copy of the entries on the register was the date on which the copy of the entries had been issued by the Land Registry. Matthew now needed to know this date, as the main point of this search was to make sure that there had been no change in the register since the date when the registry had issued their office copy. Matthew had been satisfied that, on that date, everything was in order. The object of the present exercise was to make sure that nothing adverse had been entered on the register since. He was now able to copy the date into the application for his official search: 21 May 1974.

The reference on the form to: 'the last date on which the land or charge certificate was officially examined with the register' did not apply to his case: as this only applies to cases where the buyer did not receive from the seller an office copy from the Land Registry.

He indicated on the form (by putting X in the appropriate box) that: 'the written authority of the registered proprietor (or his solicitors) to inspect the register accompanies this application'. This authority to inspect the register had been sent to Matthew by Dodds & Son with their letter of 24 June, immediately after exchange of contracts, and it now came into its own. It was essential: without the written authority of Mr Timms, the Land Registry would not provide a search certificate. Matthew posted it with form 94A by first class post to the district Land Registry at Tunbridge Wells. He sent no money with the application. This is a service provided free.

LAND CHARGES SEARCH

Another official search which a buyer may be asked to make, in addition to the one made on form 94A, is a search in the Land Charges Registry, which is in Plymouth and is quite distinct from the Land Registry at Lincoln's Inn Fields, London, and the district registries. The Land Charges Register is really meant only for cases where the title to a property is unregistered, but sometimes a building society asks for a search to be made in it by the buyer, even though the property has a registered title. This is because such a search will reveal whether the buyer has been made bankrupt, something the search on form 94A at the Land Registry will not reveal. A building society may like to know if someone to whom it is about to lend some thousands of pounds is a bankrupt.

The form on which application is made to the Land Charges Registry is form K16. The only information sought is whether or not the buyer is bankrupt. The name, address and description of the buyer(s) must be filled in; there are columns in the form for this. A Land Registry stamp (from main post offices) for 50p for each name searched, is stuck on the duplicate of the form, which will be returned by the Land Charges Registry. In theory, it takes only three days for the form to be returned. In practice, it can take much longer due to delays in the registry and the post. Therefore, allow up to a fortnight to ensure that completion will not have to be postponed. The Land Charges Registry's telephone number for enquiries is Plymouth 779831.

The Forthright Building Society had not asked Matthew to supply this Land Charges search, so he did not intend to apply for one. If he had been asked to do so, now would have been the time to send off the application for it.

While he was filling forms, he thought he might as well fill in the other two, form A4 and the L.V.A. form, that would have to be ready to be handed over to Hodgson, Green & Co. at completion.

FORM A4

Form A4 is the form on which a new owner applies to the Land Registry to have his name entered as the registered proprietor. Form A4 is officially known as 'Application to register dealings with the *whole* of land comprised in registered titles', and often unofficially referred to as 'Land Registry cover'. It is not a difficult form to complete. It has four pages, but Matthew was only concerned with pages 1 and 4; the two middle pages are for use by the Land Registry.

Form A4 provided a space for the county or London borough in which the property was situated, and the title number. Then there was a space to state the 'Nature and priority of applications'. The word priority in this context refers to the order in which the applications are asked to be dealt with. Matthew was really making three separate applications, as there were three distinct alterations that would have to be made to the existing register.

First, the removal, or discharge, of Mr Timms's mortgage; secondly, Matthew's name would have to be substituted for Mr Timms's as the name of the registered proprietor; thirdly, details of Matthew's mortgage to the Forthright Building Society would have to be entered in the charges register.

This part of the form, when filled in by Matthew, read as follows:

Nature and priority of applications	Value	Fee scale para. or abatement	£ p
Discharge of mortgage	—	—	—
Transfer	£16,250	4	42·50
Mortgage	£13,000	*abatement*	—

Total Land Registry fees paid £42·50

Since no Land Registry fees are payable on the discharge of a mortgage, Matthew left the second, third and fourth columns blank for the item: 'Discharge of mortgage'. The Land Registry fee for the transfer is charged according to what is officially known as 'Land Registry fee scale 4', calculated on the price of the house. So Matthew wrote the figure £16250 in the second column under 'Value', and the figure '4' (meaning 'fee scale 4') in the third column under the heading: 'Fee scale para or abatement'. In the fourth column he wrote £42·50, the fee on scale 4 for a price of £16250. In the case of the item 'Mortgage', the amount of the loan on mortgage— £13000 in this case—had to be inserted in the second column. If the mortgage is registered simultaneously with the transfer, the normal Land Registry fee for a mortgage is reduced to nil. So Matthew wrote 'abatement' in the third column, and left the last column blank. Matthew had in fact already checked the Land Registry fee as being £42·50 when Hodgson, Green & Co. had sent him a list of their deductions, with their letter of 12 July, which included this item.

The next part of the form to be filled in was headed 'Panel 1—Documents lodged herewith'. The six documents which Matthew listed were: charge certificate, form 53, transfer, search certificate on form 94A, mortgage and copy of the mortgage. It is necessary under the Land Registry rules to lodge a copy of the mortgage and he knew that Hodgson, Green & Co. would be providing a copy for this purpose. The copy of the mortgage counted as being a separate document.

Panel 1 also asked for: 'Name and address of solicitor or applicant to whom the acknowledgment of the application and all requisitions made by the Land Registry including requests for unpaid fees are to be sent'. The person applying to be registered as owner (in this case Matthew) is not necessarily the one who sends or lodges the application to the registry (in this case, Hodgson, Green & Co. on behalf of the Forthright Building Society). What, in effect, the form was asking at this point was: 'Who are your building society's solicitors?'. Matthew filled in: Hodgson, Green & Co.

It can happen that a document lodged with an application to the Land Registry has to be returned to someone other than the building society's solicitors after the Land Registry has dealt with the application. This is more likely to be the case when the existing title number covers more than one property. But when a person is buying a secondhand house with a registered title from an owner occupier, no question of that usually arises. And so it was here. Accordingly, Matthew left blank the whole of panel 2 of the form, which is provided in case any documents have to be returned to someone other than the solicitor lodging the application (in this case Hodgson, Green & Co.).

On the back of the form, panel 3 asked for the full postal address of the 'new proprietor of the land' and of the 'new proprietor of a charge' to be entered on the register. Matthew was about to become the new proprietor— that is the registered owner—of the property and after 26 July his address would be the house he was now in process of buying. So he filled in 14 Twintree Avenue, Minford, Surrey, there. He also filled in the registered office address of the Forthright Building Society, the proprietor of the charge arising from the present transaction.

Panel 4 of form A4 deals with joint ownership. It quite frequently happens that a property is transferred to two or more people jointly. Often the property is transferred into the joint names of husband and wife, especially where they are providing the purchase price jointly. All the Land Registry wishes to know, where the transfer is to two or more people jointly, is: can the survivor of them give a valid receipt for capital money (that is, the proceeds if he should sell) arising on a disposition (that is, a sale) of the land? Where the property is held by them as joint tenants, that is, the share of the first to die is to pass automatically to the survivor, the answer to the question asked in panel 4 of form A4 is 'Yes'. Where it is a tenancy in common, the answer is generally 'No'.

There was no joint ownership in Matthew's case, so he left panel 4 blank.

Panel 5 dealt with a case where a limited company would be buying, or lending money on mortgage. Panel 6 applies where a mortgage is finally paid off. Neither of these circumstances was the case here. So Matthew left these two panels blank. At the bottom was a space to fill in the amount of the Land Registry fee again—£42·50—and to sign the form. Matthew enclosed a cheque for the fee of £42·50.

L.V.A. FORM

The L.V.A. form, officially form 'Stamps L(A)451', sometimes also referred to as a P.D. ('Particulars Delivered') form, asked for the particulars of the transaction which had to be given for the benefit of the Inland Revenue. This form is not obtainable from Oyez shops, but from head post offices, or from Inland Revenue stamp offices. It can be obtained by post from the Controller of Stamps office, South West Wing, Bush House, Strand, London WC2B 4QN. The form was headed, 'Particulars of Instruments transferring or leasing land'. The first item of information it sought was Description of Instrument. Matthew wondered for a frivolous moment whether it would ever be noticed if his reply to this had been: 'Cello', but his courage failed and he answered 'Transfer'. The date of the instrument he left blank for the time being—it would be filled in at completion. The form also asked for the name and address of the transferor or lessor (Mr Timms), and for the name and address of the transferee or lessee (Matthew).

'Situation of the land' had to be stated; Matthew simply wrote: '14 Twintree Avenue, Minford, Surrey'. The rating authority was asked for. The answer in his case was Minford DC. Under 'Estate or interest transferred' Matthew said: 'Freehold'. Had it been a leasehold house, Matthew would have to state 'Remainder of . . . . . years' lease from . . . . . 19 . . . . . at the rent of £ . . . . . . per annum'. The 'Consideration' he filled in as being: a capital payment of £16250; the alternatives (b) to (f) did not apply in his case. He wrote: 'nil' and 'nil' in answer to two additional questions about minerals and restrictive covenants.

Matthew signed the form and filled in his name and address, but left it undated. He would be taking it with him to completion.

COMPLETION

Completion itself was now two days away. He spoke first to Dodds & Son on the telephone and then to Hodgson, Green & Co. confirming that completion would take place on friday 26 July at 2 pm, at the offices of Messrs. Anderson, James & Pringle, 88 Great Winchester Street, Minford.

On 24 July, Matthew's official search certificate on form 94A arrived back from the Land Registry with its reassuring message: 'Since the 21st day of May 1974 NO ADVERSE ENTRY HAS BEEN MADE THEREON'. This meant that the register had not been altered since 21 May and, having seen and approved a copy of the register as it then stood, all was well so far as Matthew was concerned. The certificate was dated 23 July 1974 and under this date it said: 'Priority expires 17 August 1974'. This was the twentieth working day after the date of the issue of the certificate. It meant that Hodgson, Green & Co. would have to lodge by 17 August Matthew's application to be registered as owner.

Also on the 24 July, Matthew phoned his bank manager, and, having made the necessary arrangements previously, ordered a banker's draft for £1903·17 payable to Dodds & Son. In the evening of that day, he checked through the memorandum for completion that he had prepared for himself. He also wrote to Flint and Morgan, as a formality:

38 Broadstone Drive,
Hastings, Sussex.
26 July 1974.

Dear Sirs,
14 Twintree Avenue, Minford
Completion of my purchase of this property having today taken place, I authorise and request you to account for the deposit of £100 in your hands to Messrs. Dodds & Son, the seller's solicitors, or as they direct.

Yours faithfully,
M. J. Seaton

Messrs. Flint & Morgan.

Had the property been empty, it would have been sensible for Matthew to go and look at it the day before, or the morning of, completion to check that everything was in order and it was still unoccupied. If you do find people living there who refuse to go, you should not complete because on completion, vacant possesion must be given. You should immediately notify the seller's solicitor: this is the seller's problem. If a buyer cannot get vacant possession, clauses 22 and 23 of the National Conditions of Sale come into effect and at this stage, a buyer who is not using a solicitor should get hold of one. The buyer should also tell his bank and building society's solicitor what is happening. It can be a long drawn-out process to get rid of the squatters.

Moving day was hectic, and it was made more so by Matthew having to detach himself from the general operation and attend to complete his purchase. In the morning he went to his bank and collected the banker's draft. He had to write a cheque for it, made out to his bank, and was then handed the banker's draft by the cashier in exchange. He had to pay £1·50 for it. The banker's draft was a cheque for £1903·17 made payable to Dodds & Son and signed by the bank manager on behalf of the bank itself; a bank's cheque instead of Matthew's own, in fact, and so, to a stranger, less likely to bounce.

Matthew made sure that he took all his documents and papers with him to completion. The most vital documents, the ones he had listed to hand over at completion, he specially checked, to make sure he had them with him.

He was the first to arrive at the offices of Anderson, James & Pringle, the firm acting for Mr Timms's building society, the Minford Building Society. Next to arrive was Mr Jones, a clerk employed by Dodds & Son (Mr Timms's solicitors) and the last to arrive was a man from Hodgson, Green & Co., acting for Matthew's building society, the Forthright Building Society. Nothing started until they were all there. Matthew had a vague feeling of being in the lion's den.

They were all three shown into a room rather too small for so many people, especially with the quantity of paper, in varying degrees of tidiness, stacked around the room. It was by no means a scene of Dickensian dust and disorder which solicitor's offices are sometimes imagined to be, but it was obviously a room where a great deal of paper work was done.

An articled clerk (that is, a solicitor's apprentice) represented the host firm, Anderson, James & Pringle, and he produced what he called 'the deeds'. These were in fact, not deeds but only a number of old local search certificates, requisitions and other documents, none of them now of any importance, and the charge certificate. The charge certificate was handed, via Dodds & Son, to Matthew, who opened it, verified that it related to 14 Twintree Avenue and bore the same title number as the one by reference to which they had all corresponded throughout the operation. He passed it to Hodgson, Green & Co., who also examined it briefly, then folded it up and kept it.

Next Anderson, James & Pringle produced an undertaking regarding form 53, the form which acknowledges that a building society mortgage has been paid off. It was not, apparently, the practice of the Minford Building Society to be able to hand over form 53 on the occasion of the discharge of its mortgages. The best that they could offer was to provide a written undertaking that they would send form 53 within seven days.

'To whom' asked the young man from Anderson, James & Pringle, 'shall I make out this undertaking?' looking from face to face. 'Me. Hodgson, Green & Co. Hodgson with a g and no e, if you don't mind'. Anderson, James & Pringle complied, and filled in the necessary name and address on the undertaking, then handed it to Hodgson, Green & Co. This is what it said:

Anderson, James & Pringle   *88 Great Winchester Street,*
Solicitors   *Minford, Surrey.*
                                                                      26th July, 1974.
Dear Sirs,
                     re: 14 Twintree Avenue, Minford
   As solicitors for the Minford Building Society, we hereby undertake to forward to you form 53 duly executed by the Society within seven days.
                                      Yours faithfully,
                            Anderson, James & Pringle
Hodgson, Green & Co.

Another way of dealing with this matter is for the seller's solicitors to provide the undertaking on the basis that it is the seller's responsibility to see that his mortgage is properly paid off and evidence of the paying off given to the purchaser. The form of such an undertaking is along these lines:

'In consideration of your today completing the purchase of 14 Twintree Avenue, Minford, we hereby undertake forthwith to pay over to the Minford Building Society the money required to redeem the mortgage dated 10 November 1965 and to forward Form 53 to you as soon as it is received by us from the Minford Building Society.

                                                                      Dodds & Son.'

'Transfer?' said Matthew to Dodds & Son, to show that he knew the routine. The transfer was produced. Matthew recognised it as the one he had filled in himself. It now had a red seal at the bottom, and signatures:
'Signed, sealed and delivered
by the said *William Herbert Timms*   *W. H. Timms*
in the presence of:
Name: *Roland M. Dodds*
Address: *1 Charter St, Minford, Surrey.*
Description or occupation: *Solicitor*'

Matthew copied these particulars on to his copy of the transfer. 'Shall we put today's date?' said Mr Jones of Dodds & Son, looking from Matthew to Hodgson, Green & Co. 'Yes, I think so' they all agreed, so Mr Jones took back the transfer and wrote the date—26 July 1974—in the space provided for it and then handed the transfer back to Matthew who wrote this date on his copy too, so that it was now a complete copy. This done, he handed the transfer on to Hodgson, Green and Co., who glanced at it, and kept it.

'I must execute the mortgage now and you will be witnessing it. Is that right?' Matthew asked Hodgson, Green & Co.

'That's right.'

Matthew produced the mortgage deed, and signed it at the end, alongside the part where it said: 'Signed, sealed and delivered by the said Matthew John Seaton in the presence of . . .'. The man from Hodgson, Green & Co. added his name, address and occupation in the space provided for the witness. The deed was then dated. There was a blank space in the middle of the deed for the date when the first monthly payment was to be made. This was filled in, and then the mortgage deed was complete. Hodgson, Green & Co. retained it with the other documents. Matthew entered the details in his copy of the mortgage deed, the one that he would be keeping, so that his copy would be a complete one. He might need to refer to it in the future.

Matthew now handed to Hodgson, Green & Co. his Land Registry application form (form A4) and the L.V.A. form; both of these forms had been filled in by him beforehand, except for the date, which he now added. Finally, he produced his official search certificate from the Land Registry on form 94A, which showed that no adverse entries on the register had been made since 21 May 1974; a clear search, as it is sometimes called. Hodgson, Green & Co. had made their own search also, because they were going to have a mortgage on the property. Not every building society bothers to do this. Matthew nevertheless had to hand over his search certificate, because this would be needed at the registry when his application to be registered as owner was being dealt with there.

Dodds & Son produced receipts for the current half-year's rates and water rates and Matthew compared the figures shown on them with those on the completion statement; the figures agreed. He handed the receipts back to Dodds & Son.

'Have you the keys, please?' asked Matthew. 'Oh yes, I have them here,' said Mr Jones, and produced an envelope containing three front door keys, one formidable looking back door key, and one key to the garage. 'There used to be two keys to the garage, but one's got lost, apparently,' said Mr Jones. Keys are sometimes left with the estate agents. If this had happened here, Matthew would at this point have received a written authority from Dodds & Son addressed to Flint and Morgan, asking them to hand the keys to Matthew.

Anderson, James & Pringle, and also Dodds & Son, were now waiting for their money. Matthew produced from a large envelope his banker's draft for £1903·17. He handed it to Dodds & Son, who inspected it carefully and wrote down the amount on a bit of paper.

Hodgson, Green & Co. now produced two banker's drafts, and handed them both to Matthew. This was the correct procedure, as they (or rather their client, the Forthright Building Society) were doing business only with Matthew, and with no one else present. Matthew examined the drafts. They were as they should be: one for £3738·07 payable to the Minford Building Society, the other for £9027·36 was payable to Dodds & Son. Matthew handed both drafts to Dodds & Son; he had no direct relationship with the Minford Building Society, so he did not hand the one for £3738·07 to Anderson, James & Pringle. Dodds & Son checked the two drafts. The figure of £9027·36 was added to the £1903·17 on the bit of paper. The total was £10930·53, and this was the right figure. Dodds & Son handed the banker's draft for £3738·07 to Anderson, James & Pringle, who checked it and nodded assent. Completion was over; there had been no hitches.

The usual courtesies ended the proceedings, just as they had begun them. Matthew hurried away, in the hope of getting to the house, now safely his, ahead of the moving lorry.

AFTER COMPLETION

That was the end of the legal formalities for Matthew. But it would not have been, had the property been leasehold. The buyer must usually notify the landlord's solicitor that the lease has been transferred to the buyer. Some leases demand that the transfer itself should be produced to the landlord's solicitor for inspection and return. Even if it does, the buyer need only send a copy of the transfer. If the lease requires that the landlord should be notified of the change of ownership and no more, the buyer merely has to write a letter to the landlord's solicitor, saying: 'The property known as .... comprised in the lease dated .... for a term of .... years was transferred on .... to .... of ....'. It is usual to send a notification like this in duplicate, getting the landlord's solicitor to sign an acknowledgment on the copy and sent it back as proof that the buyer has honoured this clause in the lease. There is usually a fee of a few pounds, which, under the same clause in the lease, the landlord's solicitor can demand for noting the transfer of ownership; this the buyer must pay.

All the formalities that remained in connection with Matthew's purchase would be dealt with by Hodgson, Green & Co., but if he had had no mortgage he would have dealt with them himself. The transfer would be stamped in the course of the next few days. This would be done either at one of the stamp offices, or through a head post office. There are stamp offices of the Inland Revenue in London, Birmingham, Bristol, Cardiff, Leeds, Liverpool, Manchester, Newcastle, Nottingham and Sheffield, where one can attend personally and produce the deeds for stamping. The procedure at the stamp office is to go to one counter where the deeds are each officially marked in pencil with the amount of the stamp duty. This done, the deeds have to be taken to a window in the office where the stamp duty is actually paid. Payment is usually made in cash. A seal representing the amount of duty paid is then embossed in red on each deed. Next, the form L(A) 451—the particulars delivered form—is handed in to another official, and another stamp is marked on the transfer to show that the required particulars about the transaction have been delivered to the Inland Revenue. It is possible to send deeds for stamping through the post, using form Stamps 61 (obtainable from head post offices) which has to be completed and sent to The Controller of Stamps, Inland Revenue (D), (Direct Post Section), West Block, Barrington Road, Worthing, West Sussex, with the deeds and payment for the correct amount of stamp duty.

The final stage in the legal side of buying a house is for the buyer to apply to be registered as the owner at the Land Registry. In Matthew's case this would be done by Hodgson, Green & Co., who would bundle all the documents together and send them by post to the district land registry at Tunbridge Wells as soon as they received form 53 from Anderson, James & Pringle. They would send: the charge certificate, form 53 executed by the Minford Building Society, the transfer from Mr Timms to Matthew, the mortgage by Matthew to the Forthright Building Society, a certified copy of this mortgage, the official search certificate on form 94A, form A4 signed by Matthew and a cheque for £42·50 for the Land Registry fees. These would be acknowledged by the Land Registry by return of post. If for some reason there had been a delay and form 53 had not arrived, the application to register Matthew as owner should have been sent to the Land Registry without it, so that the application would have reached there not later than 17 August, twenty working days from the date of the official search certificate on form 94A. Form 53 could then have been sent on later.

The Land Registry would register Matthew as owner within a few weeks. A new charge certificate will be prepared. The register would not show Mr Timms as the owner, nor will it show an existing mortgage to the Minford Building Society. Instead, it will show Matthew John Seaton of 14 Twintree Avenue, Minford, Surrey, school teacher, as the new registered proprietor and, in the charges register, it will show a charge to the Forthright Building Society. The charge certificate in this form will be sent to Hodgson, Green & Co., who will check it, and send it to their clients, the Forthright Building Society, who will keep it. They will keep it as security for the loan until Matthew has finished paying off the mortgage, or until he comes to sell the house, when the whole cycle will start again.

Matthew's conveyancing responsibilities had ended on the day of completion. However, just to prove to himself, if to no one else, that his object had been accomplished, Matthew thought he would like to acquire a copy of the entries on the register in its new form, showing him as the registered proprietor.

Three months after completion, Matthew filled in Land Registry form A.44 which he had obtained right back at the beginning of the transaction. The form is called 'Application for Office Copies'. He wrote in the circle by 'Register entries' the number of copies he wanted (one, in his case), and in the section below, put an X in the square declaring 'I am the registered proprietor'. He enclosed a cheque for 75p, although he could have bought Land Registry stamps from the post office, and sent the form off to Tunbridge Wells without a covering letter.

When Matthew received the copy of the entries on the register a few days later, he found that, sure enough, he was shown in the proprietorship register as being the owner of the house.

SELLING

Selling is on the whole easier than buying, from the legal standpoint. All that has to be obtained is money—the selling price. When buying, it is necessary to find out and verify all sorts of things, and to bring about successfully various legal consequences and it is not always obvious whether or not these have been achieved at the end of the transaction. When selling, if you end up with the cash, you know that you have succeeded in what you set out to do.

This does not mean that you can just sit back and wait for the money. You will have to provide the answers to some tricky questions the buyer will ask. And in several respects the seller has to take the initiative; he has to prepare the draft contract, for instance.

ESTATE AGENTS

The first step is to find a buyer. There is nothing to stop you trying to sell your house without an estate agent if you want to. You can advertise in the press, put up a notice outside the house and tell your friends. The estate agent's commission which you will save, if you succeed in finding a buyer this way, can be considerable. But estate agents have contacts, and may well be able to put you in touch with someone willing to buy.

If the house is put into the hands of an estate agent, he should set out in writing what he will do and how much he will charge, in order to earn his commission. Normally, an estate agent should receive a commission only if he introduced the buyer who actually completes the purchase. Any wording in anything he asks you to sign such as '. . . payable on our introducing a buyer ready, willing and able to buy . . .' should not be accepted. Nor should you agree to the estate agent having 'sole selling rights', as this might mean that he would be entitled to be paid a commission even when you sold your house to the friend of a friend, not introduced by the agent. There may, however, be an advantage in agreeing to a 'sole agency'. This means that you agree not to put the house into the hands of any other estate agents. But it is best for this to be for a limited period, say, a month.

Some estate agents are members of bodies such as the Royal Institution of Chartered Surveyors, or the Incorporated Society of Valuers and Auctioneers. Some have a scale as the basis for the payment of commission on the sale of houses: 2½ per cent (plus VAT) on the first £5000 of the selling price, and 1½ per cent on the rest. But estate agents are not obliged to charge on this scale. Each firm is free to charge what it likes, and the various professional institutions cannot prevent firms from undercutting the scale. Other firms operate a sliding scale, charging, say, 1½ per cent, 2 per cent or 2½ per cent of the selling price of the house (plus VAT).

Estate agents who belong to these and some other professional organisations participate in a scheme designed to protect deposits. In the case of an estate agent becoming bankrupt or defaulting, the buyer and seller of the house are refunded any deposit held by the estate agent.

There is nothing to stop you shopping around to find the agent who will do the best job for the cheapest rate. Beware of unqualified and unknown firms, however, who may be unreliable.

DEEDS AND DOCUMENTS

Selling is the mirror image of buying. The detailed description of how 14 Twintree Avenue, Minford came to be transferred from William Timms to Matthew Seaton necessarily involved a detailed description of what Dodds & Son, the seller's solicitors, had to do. In selling, as in buying, circumstances vary greatly, and in what follows, only the sale of a house which is not newly-built, and the title to which is already registered at the Land Registry, is described.

If a solicitor acted for you when you bought your house, but you now intend to sell it without a solicitor, write to him for all his old papers. Provided that all the legal fees have been paid, you are entitled to be sent all your documents in the solicitor's file, except notes prepared by the solicitor for his own benefit and letters written to him by you. There is, of course, no reason why you should not have asked for them immediately after completion, when you bought.

Where there is no existing mortgage on the property—the mortgage payments may have all been made, or perhaps there never was a mortgage—you must first get hold of the deeds. You may have them in the house already, in a safe, maybe. Alternatively, you may have kept them in a bank or with the solicitors who acted for you when you bought the house. Whoever has them will have to let you have them. You will probably have to give a receipt for them. Although everybody will probably refer to them as 'the deeds', in fact what is needed is the land certificate. There may or may not be a number of old deeds—now no longer needed—which are kept with the land certificate. But when people speak of 'the deeds', in the case of registered property they mean the land certificate plus, if leasehold, the lease.

If there is an existing mortgage, there will be a charge certificate instead of there being a land certificate. In this case, it is no good asking the building society, or whoever else has the mortgage, for the charge certificate. They insist on keeping it until they are paid in full. There is no problem, however, because you do not need the actual charge certificate, only the title number, which the building society will let you know on request.

You need to know the title number at this early stage in order to apply to the Land Registry for a copy of the entries on the register. Even if you have the land certificate in your possession (there being no mortgage) you will need a copy of the entries to send to the buyer's solicitor. It saves time if you apply for and obtain a copy of the entries on the register even before a buyer has been found. It is something you can do as soon as the house is put up for sale.

There is a special form (A.44) for applying for this, called 'Application for Office Copies'. On the sale of a house, you should apply for a 'Complete set' by putting the number you require in the appropriate circle. Only you and people with your permission may apply for a copy of the register, or make official searches there. If you ask for two copies of the entries on the register, you will make sure that you will always have one copy for your file throughout the transaction while the other copy has been sent to the buyer's solicitor.

The Land Registry fee in normal cases for supplying a complete set of the entries on the register is £2·25. This can be paid by cheque or postal order or by means of special Land Registry stamps which may be bought from head post offices. Postage stamps will not do. You buy Land Registry stamps for the corrent sum and stick them in the space provided on the form and then send it to whichever of the Land Registries governs the area in which the house is. After a few days, the copy of the entries on the register will arrive by post.

THE CONTRACT

The next stage in the sale is the preparation of the draft contract. This is the document which, when signed by buyer and seller, commits them to proceed with the transaction. It is distinct from the document by which the ownership is actually transferred to the buyer, which, in the case of registered land, is called a transfer. The contract is the exchange of binding written promises to buy and sell. There is no need to wait until a buyer has been found before starting to prepare the contract; prepare as much as you can in advance. When, subsequently, you agree provisional terms with a buyer, all you will have to do is to fill in details of the price and his name and send the draft contract straightaway to him or his solicitor.

Dodds & Son, in preparing the contract for the sale of 14 Twintree Avenue, used the National Conditions of Sale as the basis for their contract. They might well have used the Law Society's Conditions of Sale. But, for the layman selling his house without a solicitor, either of these courses is usually impossible. These forms—the National Conditions and the Law Society's Conditions—are copyright. Without permission, it is illegal to reproduce the forms yourself. It also means that we cannot reproduce them for you here in this book. The printed forms are sold by law stationers, but law stationers will not sell them to laymen; only solicitors may buy them.

The forms which solicitors use have printed, in the middle two pages, standard clauses governing the details of the sale. The rest of the form is laid out so that particulars of any transaction can be completed and the form used as a contract for that sale. A contract in this style incorporates the conditions printed in the middle pages. A layman who cannot buy these forms can prepare his own contract and incorporate the National Conditions of Sale simply by reference to them, without reproducing them.

To prepare a contract, start with an ordinary piece of blank paper. You need to write or type out a number of clauses setting out the essential terms of the contract. Here is a specimen of a contract for the sale of a house:

CONTRACT FOR THE SALE OF A HOUSE WITH A REGISTERED TITLE

The seller agrees to sell and the buyer agrees to buy the house described overleaf. The name and address of the seller and of the buyer and the price agreed appear overleaf. The sale is subject to the following conditions:

1. A deposit of ten per cent of the price is to be paid. If estate agents are acting, the deposit will be held by them as stakeholders. If not, the deposit is to be held in a joint account to be opened in the name of the seller and of the buyer or his solicitors at the branch of the bank stated overleaf. Cheques drawn on the account must be signed by both parties.

2. The seller is selling as beneficial owner.

3. Copies of the property register, the charges register and of the plan have already been supplied to the buyer. The seller shall now supply a copy of the remaining entries on the register, and an authority to inspect the register.

4. Vacant possession will be given on completion, the date for which is stated overleaf. If the buyer takes possession with the consent of the seller before completion, he will be an occupier under licence for the time being, must pay interest at the rate stated overleaf on the price less deposit, and will be liable for the upkeep of the house and for the rates, insurance and other outgoings.

5. The property is used as a dwellinghouse in the occupation of one family, and this is what is permitted under the Town and Country Planning Acts.

6. The property is sold subject to and with the benefit of all rights and duties including restrictive covenants described in the property and charges registers.

7. The current edition of the National Conditions of Sale shall apply to this contract.

(Back of form of contract)

Seller's full name...
address..
....
Buyer's full name...
address..
....
Description of the property: freehold/leasehold house
   known as...
....
Price.. pounds (£   )

The property is registered at the Land Registry with title absolute/good
leasehold title under title number......................................

Leasehold only: date of lease....................................
made between..........................and..
original term of the lease...............years from...............................
number of years now unexpired....................................
ground rent £.........per year. Copy of the lease herewith.
Insurance company...
address..
policy number...................................sum for which insured £.........
annual premium £.........date for renewal...........

Bank to hold deposit in joint names...
address..
Rate of interest..............per cent per annum.
Buyer's solicitors...
address..
Completion date...
Signed.. date.................

It should be easy to fill in the blanks in this suggested form of contract. The kind of title with which the property is registered—title absolute or good leasehold title—is printed at the heading to the proprietorship register. Both the charges register and the proprietorship register are part of the copy of the entries on the register which you will have received by applying on form A44 to the Land Registry.

Where the property is leasehold, you have to send a copy of the lease to the buyer's solicitor with the draft contract. The building society's solicitors should let you have a copy (they will probably charge you for it), if you do not have a copy of your own. If there is no existing mortgage, you will have the lease (it will amost certainly be with the land certificate), and you can arrange to have it copied yourself: a photocopy is always better, but a typed copy will do. The particulars of the lease that have to be given in the draft contract all appear in the lease itself. Particulars of insurance, required only in the case of a contract for the sale of a leasehold property, can be obtained from the last receipt for the premium. Alternatively, the building society or the insurance company can provide this information.

If the buyer is found through estate agents, a small deposit may be held by them until the sale is completed. There is no rule that this must be so, however. You may suggest opening a special joint account at a bank. Your own bank would do, and so would the buyer's solicitor's bank. Such an account could be in the joint names of the seller and the buyer, or, more likely, the seller and the buyer's solicitor. The arrangement about drawing money from this joint account should be that both parties must sign cheques. The deposit is paid into this account by the buyer and stays there until the sale is completed. Later, instead of handing over a letter releasing the deposit, as would happen if estate agents were involved as stakeholders, the buyer's solicitor hands over a cheque drawn on the joint account signed by the buyer, or by his solicitor. Then all the seller has to do is to sign the cheque as well, and present it for payment to himself in the usual way. The joint account is then closed.

It is usual to leave the completion date blank in the draft contract. It will be filled in when contracts are exchanged.

It sometimes happens that the buyer takes possession of the property before completion, even immediately after exchange of contracts. The seller would be extremely foolish, of course, to let the buyer into possession before exchange of contracts. Even if the buyer has signed a binding contract, he should not be allowed to take possession, because it is sometimes found that once a buyer is in possession, he is less anxious to hurry up and complete his purchase than he would have been if he had not been allowed to get in until after completion. Worse still, a seller might be unable to regain possession of a house from a buyer who was allowed in before completion, but who refuses or is unable to complete his purchase.

If the buyer takes possession before completion of the purchase, he has to pay the rates, the water rates, and any other outgoings from the date he takes possession. In addition, he has to pay interest on the amount of the purchase price less the deposit. This is for the period from the date when he takes possession until the date when he hands over the balance of the purchase money. The interest is in place of the rent which the seller might have expected to receive for allowing the buyer to occupy the property without paying the purchase money. About 3 to 5 per cent above the current building society mortgage interest rate is a fair average of what a buyer would have to pay in the circumstances.

The one thing which the seller is usually anxious to keep to himself until contracts are exchanged is the price at which he bought the property, especially if he bought it comparatively recently. This is usually because, if he were to reveal it, the buyer might have second thoughts about the price he is offering to pay. As the price the seller paid may be on the proprietorship register, part of the copy of the entries on the register extracted from the Land Registry, the seller normally does not show the whole of the proprietorship register to the buyer until after exchange of contracts. Until then, the practice is not to show the buyer any of the register entries except a copy of the restrictive covenants, as set out in the charges register. But there is really no reason why the buyer should not be sent, before contracts are exchanged, the whole of the property register, the filed plan and the charges register, leaving undisclosed, at this stage, the price the seller paid. This can be done by snipping off the copy which the buyer is sent.

The form suggested for a draft contract provides that copies of the property register, the filed plan and the charges register should be sent with the draft contract. The advantage is that if, by any chance, the seller misunderstood some aspect of the matter, or inaccurately transposed the information given in the register in filling in the draft contract, any such errors will be obvious to the buyer's solicitor before contracts are exchanged, so that he cannot complain later that he was misled by the way in which the contract was worded. By doing it this way, you would, in effect, be saying: 'Here is the register of the property from the Land

Registry (except for the middle part, the proprietorship register); this sets out what I am selling and what it is subject to. You can see for yourself what is involved'. In this way, the risk of misdescribing something, or of leaving out something important when preparing the draft contract, is considerably reduced. After contracts are exchanged, you will need to send to the buyer's solicitor only the copy of the proprietorship register, together with an authority to inspect the register. The rest he will already have received.

The draft contract is now ready to be sent to the buyer's solicitor. It is normal to send it with a copy for his use. He will keep one copy and send the other back with his amendments and comments.

ENQUIRIES BEFORE CONTRACT

At about this stage in the transaction, you will be faced with answering enquiries before contract, or preliminary enquiries, as they are often called, which the buyer's solicitor will probably send you immediately after he has received from you the draft contract. They are most likely to be in the standard printed form, form Conveyancing 29 (Long) published by Oyez Publishing Ltd.

Answering questions is usually more difficult than asking them, especially when all that is involved in asking is buying a form on which they are all printed. Solicitors have a technique for answering these questions. Dodds & Son used this when answering the questions which Matthew Seaton asked in his enquiries before contract. Typical answers are: 'There are none of which the vendor is aware, but the sale is made subject to any there might be', 'Your local searches should reveal this', 'Inspection will show' and even 'We cannot say'. The seller is under no duty, as a matter of law, to volunteer anything he knows about the property, or its past or its future. It is therefore necessary for the buyer to ask a number of questions. The seller need not answer them, but if he does, he must not tell lies. Neither must be—even innocently—misrepresent any facts.

Some of the questions in the preliminary enquiries may appear a little farfetched, perhaps. Some may seem wholly inappropriate for the situation. But the form has been devised to cover as wide a field as possible. You may feel like saying 'What utter nonsense; of course not' to some questions, but there is a reason for every one of them. Many of the questions use legal language and you may have some difficulty in understanding what they mean. If so, there is no harm in saying so. 'I do not understand this question' is an honest answer. The buyer's solicitor may not pursue the question. On the other hand, he may ask the same question again, only this time in plain english.

Where you have obtained the papers which were used by your solicitors when you bought the house, you should find with them the preliminary enquiries then asked, together with the answers then given. These should help with the answers to some of the questions now being asked, although you may find that the order and layout of the questions on the form have changed since you bought the house.

The solicitor acting for the buyer is not likely to be particularly sympathetic towards any difficulties you may have in trying to answer his preliminary enquiries. On the other hand, he is primarily interested in getting sufficiently detailed information from you to enable him to fulfil his duty to his client. If you are really lost in trying to answer the questions, you are at liberty to write or phone the buyer's solicitor and say: 'I cannot make head or tail of the form you sent me. I will give you any information I can about the house, but you will have to help me to understand what you want to know. I suggest that I come along to your office and I'll bring all my papers.' The buyer's solicitor cannot force you to answer the questions—you are under no legal obligation to provide this information. But it is the practice to give it, and you may find, if you do not provide satisfactory answers to his questions, that he will advise his client, the buyer, not to go through with the proposed purchase, and as a result you may lose a sale.

Finally, you may find that trying to wrestle with providing answers to the preliminary enquiries is too much for you altogether, in which case you may decide that there is more to conveyancing than you had thought. You will then have to place the matter in the hands of a solicitor.

After the anguish of answering the preliminary enquiries, you are likely to have a lull. During this period the house may be surveyed for the buyer and for his building society, and his solicitor will be making his local search and fixing up the insurance, perhaps. They will all be pretty active, in fact, while you may be sitting back waiting for something to happen. It is during this period that there may be some correspondence between you and the buyer's solicitor about the draft contract. He may urge that the contract be framed quite differently from what you suggested. On the other hand, he may accept your basis. It is generally up to the seller to determine the terms on which he will sell. The buyer's solicitor may suggest the addition or alteration of one or two clauses to cover various points. But in the sale of a secondhand house with a registered title there should be little difficulty in agreeing the form of the contract. If the buyer encounters difficulty in getting a mortgage, or in selling his house, there may well be delay and frustration at this stage. If this goes on, you will eventually have to decide whether to continue with this sale or, instead, to put the house back on the market. There is no contract yet to tie either seller or buyer.

Before preparing the engrossment of the contract (the piece of paper you will actually sign), be quite sure that it is in the form which both you and the buyer's solicitor have agreed. It often happens that no amendments are made, so that the draft contract itself can be used for the engrossment. If there are amendments, however, first in red ink, and then counter-amendments, in green perhaps, the draft contract is unlikely to be suitable for use as an engrossment. In that case you will have to prepare a clean copy for signature. Each side prepares a separate engrossment and signs a separate contract. The one the buyer signs is sent to the seller and the one the seller signs is sent to the buyer. Each should read exactly the same.

BRIDGING LOANS
The same person is often the seller of one house and the buyer of another. Because of this, a number of transactions can all be linked to form a chain: Mr A selling The Limes to Mr B, Mr B selling 19 Acacia Avenue to Mr C, Mr C selling Mon Repos to Mr D, and so on. Some nice timing is sometimes called for in this situation. Most people in the chain are relying on the proceeds of the house being sold to help pay for the house being bought. It would be unwise for a person to commit himself to his purchase until he has received a signed contract in respect of his sale. Take Mr B for instance; if he were to commit himself to buying The Limes before he had received a signed contract from Mr C for the sale of 19 Acacia Avenue, he would be in danger of being unable, through lack of funds, to fulfil his promise to buy The Limes: Mr C may never sign the contract and it may then turn out to be difficult to sell 19 Acacia Avenue to someone else, except after a delay or at a reduced price. Everyone, therefore, ought to hold back from signing a contract to buy a house until he has received a binding contract for the house he is selling. A whole series of transactions can reach stagnation in this way, with everyone waiting about for one man to take the plunge. When he does, the rest of them can follow in rapid succession.

One way to break the deadlock is by arranging a temporary loan from a bank to bridge the gap between buying and selling. This is called a bridging loan. The bank lends enough to enable someone to buy the new house, and when his present house is sold, the bridging loan is repaid. Before negotiating for a bridging loan, find out if your bank charges an arrangement (or commitment) fee, for arranging such a loan, even if, finally, it is not taken up.

Often a bank will only provide a bridging loan for a customer after he has obtained a signed contract for the house he is selling. Even so, a bridging loan can be useful. It can bridge the gap between different completion dates. It is often difficult, if not impossible, fully to co-ordinate the completion dates of the two transactions in which one person is involved, the buying and the selling. Where it proves impossible, there will be a gap between the one and the other. There is no problem where the sale is completed first, followed by a gap, after which the purchase is completed. The proceeds from the sale can then be used to complete the purchase, having, perhaps, earned a bit of interest in the meantime, while on deposit at the bank during the gap. But where the purchase is completed first, and then later the sale is completed, the problem arises of finding the money to complete the purchase at a time when the money from the sale is not yet available. It is here that the bank may help with a bridging loan.

A bank may hesitate to provide a bridging loan for a buyer acting without a solicitor. The reason is that normally the bank obtains from the solicitor a personal undertaking to pay the funds to the bank on completion, and in the meantime to hold any deeds on behalf of the bank. In this context, a solicitor's undertaking is a special protection to the bank; a layman's undertaking is not as good from their point of view. Whether an individual can get round the problem depends on his relationship with the bank manager. If you do manage to get a loan from the bank, make sure that when the loan is granted it is expressed in such terms as will make it eligible for tax relief (an ordinary bank overdraft is not).

Co-ordination of buying and selling can be quite tricky, especially where it is vital to use the money from the sale to pay for the purchase. The golden rule is never to bind yourself by signing a contract to buy a house, until you are sure of being able to pay for it. Money of your own, or loans (bridging, mortgage, or others), or the proceeds of sale of a house which someone has signed a contract to buy from you, or a combination of these three sources, should provide the means of doing so.

EXCHANGE OF CONTRACTS

When the contract itself is ready for signature, it must be signed. The seller is generally ready to exchange contracts before the buyer. You may find therefore, that you are left sitting around with your engrossment, waiting to hear from the buyer's solicitor with the contract signed by the buyer. Do not overlook the possibility that you will receive, not the contract but the news that the buyer is not going through with his proposed purchase after all. Until you receive a contract signed by the buyer, there is no binding contract. He does not have to give any reason for withdrawing.

In most cases, however, the day comes when the contract signed by the buyer arrives by post. The custom is for the buyer to send his part to the seller first. At the same time, the buyer should pay the deposit, or the balance of it—to the solicitor or into the joint account, as the case may be—unless he has already done so. It often happens that the deposit, or at least part of it, is paid well before exchange of contracts.

It is quite normal for the contract signed by the buyer to be sent without being dated. If this happens, it is intended that you, the seller, should date it with the day on which you receive it. You should then date with the same date that part of the contract which you signed and which you will send in exchange. In the same way, you may have to fill in the space left for the date for the completion of the sale. This date—usually four weeks later—may have been agreed at the last minute between both sides on the telephone.

You now send the contract signed by yourself to the buyer's solicitor. With it you send the rest of the copy of the entries on the register, that is to say, any part of it which the buyer's solicitor has not already received. If you have retained just the proprietorship register, you send it now. You may, on the other hand, have so far sent only a copy of the restrictive covenants affecting the property, in which case you will now have to send, not only the proprietorship register, but also the property register, and the remainder of the charges register. One way or another, now is the time to put the buyer's solicitor in the position of holding a complete copy of the entries on the register.

The other document which you must now send is an authority to inspect the register. There is a printed form you can use for this. It is form 201 and can be obtained from the Oyez shops. It is quite easy to fill in, and has to be signed by you as registered proprietor. It has to be worded so as to allow the buyer's solicitor to inspect the register. He needs an authority to inspect the register in order to make an official search just before completion. You do not need to use the printed form, however. An ordinary letter, addressed to the Land Registry, will do. It might read like this:

135 Thackeray Villas,
Picklebridge, Lancs.
27th July, 1974.

Dear Sir,

Title No. LA24689753
135 Thackeray Villas, Picklebridge

Please permit Messrs. Forbes, Wainwright & Spencer, solicitors, of Bank Chambers, High Street, Blakeford to inspect the register relating to the above title.

Yours faithfully,
Herbert Reginald Oakes
(registered proprietor)

The Chief Land Registrar,
The Lytham District Land Registry,
Lytham St. Annes,
Lancs.

MORTGAGE

As soon as contracts are exchanged, you should contact your building society, or their solicitors. Before then, you could not have said for certain that you would be in a position to pay off the existing mortgage, nor could you have said when you would be able to do so. But the moment you have exchanged contracts with the buyer, you are entitled to assume that the sale will go through, and that you will be able to pay off your mortgage. Furthermore, you know when this will be: on the date for completion fixed by the contract, for this will be the day when you should receive the selling price which will enable you to pay off the mortgage.

Many mortgages contain a clause saying that you must give three months' notice of your intention to pay off the mortgage. It may be more, it may be less. This means that you have to pay interest up to a day three months (or whatever it is) following the day you first give official notice to the building society that you intend to pay off the mortgage. Accordingly, the sooner you give notice, the less you will have to pay by way of interest. The building society's concern is to obtain income from the money it lends on mortgage, a form of investment from the society's point of view. If borrowers were free to repay at a moment's notice the money they had borrowed, it might happen (in theory at least) that there would be no other person anxious to borrow that money immediately. In the meantime, therefore, until another borrower was found, the money would not be earning interest, and the society would suffer financially. To guard against this, the society demands that a borrower wishing to repay the money should give advance notice of his intention to do so, to give the society a chance to find a suitable alternative investment for the money. The borrower can always pay interest for the period of three months, or whatever it is, instead of letting the period of notice run out. In fact, this is what generally happens. But it is worth while for an owner selling his house to give notice to his building society as soon as he can, as this may save him having to pay extra interest. Obviously, the shorter the period of notice required to pay off the mortgage, the better it is from the borrower's point of view. Some building societies require a repayment fee if the mortgage is paid off in less than, say, five years from the time of borrowing.

If you have already been in contact with the building society's solicitors, all letters should be written to them, rather than to the building society. If not, write to the building society at the branch you have always dealt with. The chances are that you will hear in reply from their solicitors, anyway.

When writing, ask how much money will be required to pay off the mortgage on the day fixed for completion. You may find that the building society is prepared to accept less than the three months' interest it is entitled to demand, and may in fact only charge interest up to, say, the date of completion. When you are notified of the amount required to pay off your mortgage, check it against your last yearly statement received from the building society. The method of calculating building society interest varies; you will have to look at the mortgage deed and the rules to see which method applies.

One of the commonest methods works something like this. A calculation is made on 31 December in each year. On that day interest at the agreed rate—11 per cent, or whatever is the current rate—is calculated on the capital sum outstanding on that day, and that interest is then debited to your account. Putting it another way, a year's interest is at this time (31 December) added to the capital outstanding, to produce the total amount you then owe the building society. Throughout the next year you will be making regular payments, each of which will reduce the amount you owe. At some point in the year, a payment will bring the total you owe below the level at which the loan stood on the previous 31 December, and, for the rest of the year, each payment will reduce the outstanding capital, so that by the end of the year, the total outstanding will be so much less than it was at the previous 31 December. But then suddenly, as in the previous year, the interest for a year will be calculated again, and the amount of your debt to the building society will go shooting up again, though not up to the amount it was the year before. Each year you pay back a bit more capital than in the previous year, so that the capital outstanding gets progressively less, and thus the interest to be paid—while the interest rate remains the same—gets a little bit less also. In each of the last few years of, say, a 20 year period over which mortgage payments are spread, the repayments represent more capital than interest, whereas in the early years more interest is paid than capital.

There are several variations. Some building societies compute interest every six months, instead of every year. Sometimes no capital repayments are made while the mortgage lasts, interest only being paid. In this case, it is much easier to calculate what is required to pay off the mortgage at any time: it is just the amount of the loan plus interest at the current rate from the beginning of the current year up to the day of completion (or whenever else it is).

Something may happen to delay the agreed completion date. If so, there may have to be an adjustment in the amount the building society requires to pay off the mortgage. To anticipate this sort of possibility, the building society, as well as telling you how much money is required to pay off the mortgage on a stated day, will sometimes tell you the amount of interest that will accrue each day thereafter. If, for instance, you have asked what is required to pay off the mortgage on 17 November, the answer may be £2103·22 with interest thereafter of 33p per day. If completion were to take place two days late, on 19 November, you would have to add another 66p to the £2103·22, making £2103·88 as the amount required to pay off the mortgage on 19 November. To be told this daily rate saves having to go back to the building society for a recalculation if completion is slightly delayed, as sometimes happens.

something may happen to delay completion

REQUISITIONS ON TITLE

Shortly after exchange of contracts, the buyer's solicitor will probably send some questions called requisitions on title, and at the same time, or a little later, will send you the draft transfer deed.

The requisitions on title may be on a printed form. It is most likely to be form Con. 28B published by Oyez Publishing Ltd. If so, you will be asked to confirm that the answers you gave to preliminary enquiries still apply, and if they do not, to give particulars of any variation. 'The seller is not aware of any variation' is the usual reply.

You will also be asked to produce receipts for 'rates, taxes and outgoings' at completion. Now that receipts are generally not given for such payments unless specially asked for, this is not easy to comply with. If you have receipts, well and good. If not, you will have to get them or procure other evidence (such as a letter from the treasurer of the local council) to show what you have paid and to justify the basis on which to apportion rates—and other outgoings—in the completion statement.

You can leave question 3B(1) unanswered, as a recent office copy of the register will have been supplied by you to the buyer. Question 4 deals with mortgages, and states that all subsisting mortgages must be discharged on or before completion. This is obviously so, and should be agreed. Then it asks whether 'the vacating receipt, discharge of registered charge or consent to dealing' will be handed over on completion. So far as a secondhand house with a registered title is concerned, it is the discharge of registered charge—form 53, in fact—which applies. (The vacating receipt is the receipt for mortgage monies endorsed at the end of a mortgage of unregistered property, when it is paid off. A consent to dealing is used when an owner of several properties, a builder, for instance, has a mortgage on all of them and one is sold off, at which point the lender has to consent to the sale, freeing the property sold from his mortgage.) Building societies often do not hand over the discharge of a registered charge—form 53—at completion, but only an undertaking to do so, so the question is asked in order to get it clear what is going to happen.

Question 4(B)(ii) asks about the wording of the undertaking, if that is what is to be given. A solicitor's undertaking is something special. Provided that it is not qualified in any way, it puts the solicitor under a personal obligation to carry it out, even if, for instance, his client defaults. It is only on the basis of such an undertaking that, at completion, the buyer and his building society will be content to go away without form 53 in their hands. So its wording is important. It must be given by the solicitor personally, and be unqualified, so as to commit him. And it must require compliance within a specified period, say 7 days.

Question 5 deals with where completion is to take place and the banker's drafts that will then be required. You will probably not be able to supply this information until later, and should say so on the form.

You will be told, on the form of requisitions on title, that you must give vacant possession of the house on completion. This you already know, and indeed are, by contract, bound to do. All you need to say is: 'Agreed'. There may be some other questions, special to the circumstances of your case, which the buyer's solicitor may have added to the form. They are likely to be practical rather than legal. If you do not understand a question, by all means say so, and ask the buyer's solicitor to explain.

These requisitions on title may, instead of being on a printed form, be typed or duplicated on a piece of ordinary paper. This should present no difficulty. Here again, you may find that questions are left standing which ought really to have been struck out, either because they have already been asked, in substance, in the preliminary enquiries, in which case the reply to give is: 'See reply to question . . . . . . in enquiries before contract', or because they are inappropriate to the circumstances of the sale, such as being apt only for a sale where the title is unregistered. In such a case the reply to give is: 'Does not apply'. At the end of the requisitions on title is a space for your signature and the date. You then send the form back to the buyer's solicitor, keeping the copy for your file.

TRANSFER

The draft transfer is usually sent with the requisitions. Once more, you will probably be provided with a copy for your file and you may be invited by the buyer's solicitor to treat the top copy of the transfer (as opposed to the carbon copy) as the engrossment, the one to be executed by you and handed over at completion. It will almost invariably be on a printed form, known as 'form 19', and will follow exactly the lines of the transfer used when Matthew Seaton bought 14 Twintree Avenue. It is up to the buyer's solicitor to decide how he wants the transfer to be worded. In fact there is very little room for variation in wording, so straightforward a form is it, as a rule. Where the buyers are a husband and wife buying in their joint names, the transfer may contain clauses regulating their rights between themselves. This need not concern you, as seller, as it is up to them to settle the basis on which they will own their house. Provided that the transfer faithfully records what is happening in the transaction, you should

F

not hesitate to approve it. If you approve the draft transfer, all you need to do is to write to the buyer's solicitor saying so, retaining the top copy for use as the engrossment, and also the carbon copy of the transfer, which will be the copy for your file.

BUYER'S BUILDING SOCIETY

Having answered the buyer's solicitor's requisitions on title and approved his draft transfer, you may find that once more there is a pause, during which there is little for you, as seller, to do on the legal side of selling a house. During this time the buyer's solicitor will be in contact with the solicitors acting for the buyer's building society, or whoever else is advancing him money on mortgage. It is likely, however, that the buyer's solicitor will also be acting for the building society. This happens when the building society operates the panel system, whereby any one of a large number of solicitors throughout the country can, and does, act for a building society in conveyancing matters. If the buyer's solicitor is on the panel of the buyer's building society, this solicitor will act both for him and for his building society in this particular transaction. If this is the case, there is unlikely to be any delay at this stage. Similarly, there is no reason for any delay if the buyer is not having a mortgage.

Where different solicitors act for the buyer and for his building society, the seller sometimes finds that he gets another set of requisitions on title. These are probably the requisitions which the building society's solicitor has thought up. The buyer's solicitor may say: 'My client's mortgagees have raised the following requisitions in addition to those which you have already answered, and I shall be glad if you will let me have replies'. You may not be bound to answer these additional requisitions, as the contract, whether it adopts the National or the Law Society's Conditions of Sale, imposes a limit (14 days from when the copy of the entries on the register was finally supplied) on the time within which requisitions may be raised. It is, however, usual to answer these additional requisitions, should they be asked, if only as a courtesy.

Nothing further is required of you until the date for completion is finally determined. The contract fixed a date for completion, but sometimes this has to be changed, for one reason or another. It is essentially a matter for the parties themselves, the buyer and the seller, rather than for solicitors, to agree the date, either that fixed by the contract or another date, as the date on which completion will actually take place. Once this has been determined, you can proceed to the next stage.

PREPARING FOR COMPLETION

Dodds & Son's completion statement on the sale of 14 Twintree Avenue sets out the form which a completion statement usually takes. The amount of money which you, as seller, will require to receive at completion consists, fundamentally, of the price agreed, less any deposit already paid by the buyer, plus or minus something for a proportion of the rates and water rates. In the case of a leasehold property, ground rent, insurance and service charge are apportioned. In calculating the apportionment of these outgoings, you have to find out the date to which each has already been paid. This will be shown on the demand for the most recent payment you made. Receipts are not given for rates and water rates unless specially requested. If you know you will be selling, you should ask for receipts, because you may need to produce them at completion. Alternatively, get a letter from the local or water authority, confirming the date to which rates are paid, and the amount.

Rates, water rates and insurance are, as a rule, paid in advance, so that, when it comes to completion, each of them should be already paid up to a date later than the agreed completion date (unless there are unpaid bills for any of them). If this is the case, you must work out how much of the payment made is for the period between the date agreed for completion and the last day covered by the payment. Thus if the half-year's rates were paid by you in October, to cover the period up to the following 31 March, and the sale is being completed on 8 February, you must work out what proportion of the rates covers the period from 8 February to 31 March. This calcualtion is made on a day-to-day basis and will produce a figure which has to be added to the amount required to complete. The figure is added, not subtracted, because you, the seller, have to be reimbursed for what you have already paid out for rates for the period from 8 February to 31 March, but which is really the liability of the buyer.

Ground rent for a leasehold house is usually paid in arrears. When, for instance, a half-year's ground rent is paid on 24 June, that payment covers the period from the previous Christmas until 24 June, rather than the period from then until the next Christmas. As a result, the apportionment of ground rent is usually in favour of the buyer: that is to say, something has to be subtracted from the money needed to complete, to cover the proportion of ground rent for the period for which no ground rent has yet been paid. The calculation is made by reference to the full amount of the annual ground rent, and no deduction for income tax is made, unless the landlord lives abroad. If the buyer has been allowed to take possession before completion, the completion statement, besides apportioning the outgoings as at the date on which the buyer moved in rather than at the date of completion, now includes an item for the interest on the balance of the purchase price. It is worked out on a daily basis: so many three hundred and sixty-fifths of one year's interest at the appropriate rate per cent on the price less deposit. Income tax is not deducted in the calculation of interest.

In the case of rates, you can get the local authority to deal with the apportionment, instead of dealing with it in the completion statement. The treasurer's department will make the necessary calculation of what you must pay them or they must pay you back, to leave you having paid the rates up to the date you move out, and no further. You will be given a receipt, if you ask for it, which you will have to produce to the buyer's solicitor at completion. If the matter is dealt with in this way, no apportionment of the rates appears in the completion statement. A similar arrangement is made if the house has been standing empty for a short time, as no rates have to be paid then. The seller should have paid the rates up to the date when the house was last occupied, and produce a receipt showing this at completion. The buyer will be asked to pay rates calculated from the date he moves in.

The completion statement can be prepared now and sent to the buyer's solicitor. Send it at least a week before the date fixed for completion, to give the buyer's solicitor time to deal with any points that may arise on it. Keep a copy for yourself.

At the same time, or maybe a few days later, you will need to tell the buyer's solicitor how the amount shown in the completion statement must be split. Where you are paying off an existing mortgage, you should have found out how much money will be needed to pay off the mortgage on the date fixed for completion. You should also have asked whether the banker's draft for the amount should be made payable to the building society itself, or to its solicitors. With this information, you can work out how the completion monies must be split: so much to the building society (or its solicitors)—however much is required to pay off the existing mortgage; the remainder to be paid to yourself.

It might, however, be more complicated than that. For instance, you may be completing the purchase of another house on the same day as you are completing the sale, using whatever is left after paying off your mortgage to help pay for the house you are buying. The solicitors concerned may have asked you to pay the money you are providing at the completion of your purchase in two separate amounts. In addition, you may be having a fresh mortgage on the house you are buying and the amount to be advanced must be taken into account as well. In this situation, with sums of money coming from and going to every direction, you must try to keep calm, and work it all out step by step.

The buyer's money is probably coming from at least two sources, too—some from a building society, say, and the rest from himself, so that it will come split already. If he is having a mortgage, and you are paying one off, you may expect that the completion monies will in fact be split at least three ways, and three bankers' drafts will be produced at completion. This is what happened at the completion of Matthew Seaton's purchase of 14 Twintree Avenue.

One other point to settle is the time and place of completion. Where a mortgage is to be paid off, completion takes place at the office of the solicitors acting for the seller's building society, or other mortgagee, or it can be carried out by post. This is more convenient if buyer and seller live a long way from each other. However, a solicitor acting for a buyer may be unwilling to complete by post with a seller acting on his own behalf. If a seller has no mortgage, completion can take place at his solicitor's office, or by post. The seller decides how and where completion will take place.

The transfer deed must be executed by you, as seller. This can be done before or at completion. There is a space at the end for this, where it says: 'Signed, sealed and delivered by the said .... in the presence of ....'. Alongside is a space for your signature, and next to that is a space for the seal. A little red paper disc with a sticky back is nowadays used to represent a seal; law stationers sell them. And a kindly solicitor at completion will give you one, or sell you one, perhaps. You should sign with your ordinary signature, provided that it includes all your initials. If your full names are, for example, Margery Anne Abrahams, and you usually sign: 'Margery Abrahams', it is better to sign: 'Margery A. Abrahams' just for this once, to make it clear that you are the person whose full names appear in the transfer.

The witness to your signature should also sign, adding his or her address and occupation in the spaces provided. Occupation means that you state your job, and, according to convention, a woman who is not working gives her status—spinster, married woman, widow or feme sole. Anyone may act as witness to the seller's signature on a transfer. Having been 'signed and sealed' the deed will be 'delivered' when it is handed over to the buyer with the intention that it should operate as a transfer.

For the seller, there are no complicated preparations required for completion. Usually he has to bring along the transfer only. Where there is no mortgage, he will have to provide the land certificate as well, and the lease, if it is a leasehold house. He will have to produce evidence of having paid the rates, the water rates, and in the case of a leasehold house, the ground rent and insurance, for the buyer's solicitor to inspect, and he will have to hand over the keys.

Before completion, you should make some arrangement about the fees of the solicitors for the building society (or other mortgage) whose existing mortgage is to be paid off. These, like other building society's solicitors' fees, must, as a rule, be met by you, the borrower. There is not much work involved for the solicitors in dealing with the repayment, or redemption as it is sometimes called, of a mortgage loan. The fee which is not governed by a scale is likely to be £5–£10 or sometimes more, depending on the circumstances. You should agree the amount in advance of completion, including how they, the solicitors concerned, want you to pay it. They will probably be happy to take a cheque from you, but they may demand cash. Their fees may be included in the sum they asked to receive to pay off the mortgage, but this is not likely.

COMPLETION

Matthew Seaton's purchase of 14 Twintree Avenue was completed in a typical way. There was not a great deal which Dodds & Son, the solicitors acting for Mr Timms the seller, had to do.

The solicitors for your building society will probably start the ball rolling by handing to you the charge certificate. As they are looking to you for payment of the money you owe, they hand it to you, although they realise that you intend to hand it straight on to the buyer's solicitor. All you need to do is to examine it, to make sure it is the right one. You then pass it

to the buyer's solicitor. The same procedure usually applies to form 53, the receipt and acknowledgment from the building society that the mortgage has been paid off (or an undertaking to provide it.)

Next, you will probably hand over the transfer. This will still be undated, and you should confirm that the buyer's solicitor wishes that the transfer should bear the date on which completion is taking place. It very occasionally happens that there is a reason why the transfer should be dated some other day. By and large, however, you are wise to insist that the transfer bears the date of completion, and no other date. When you have dated the transfer, it is handed to the buyer's solicitor, who will hand it to his building society's solicitors together with the mortgage deed and any other items required.

Next, the buyer's solicitor will turn back to you and ask to inspect the last receipts (or other evidence of payment) for rates, water rates and any other outgoings apportioned in the completion statement. He does this to verify that the apportionments were made on the correct basis. If there are any outgoings which you have not yet paid, you may take this opportunity of handing over to the buyer's solicitor the demands for the sums currently due.

Then comes the money. The buyer's solicitor will produce banker's drafts totalling the amount required to complete, as set out in your completion statement. One draft will probably have come from the buyer's building society, and the rest from the buyer himself. You will have already arranged that your building society should receive the amount needed to pay off your mortgage, and you will receive the balance, in the form of a banker's draft made payable to you by name.

Sometimes it is necessary for a banker's draft to be endorsed at completion. For example, you may find that the buyer's building society produces the required banker's drafts, but that both are made payable to the buyer's solicitor, instead of one being payable to you, as seller, and the other to your building society. In this case the buyer's solicitor must endorse the drafts to make them payable to the person for whom they are ultimately intended. A banker's draft (like any other kind of cheque) may be endorsed generally, by the person or firm to whom it is made out just signing on the back of it, in which case anyone can cash it. Alternatively, it may be endorsed specially, by the person or firm to whom it is made out writing on the back: 'Pay X' or 'Pay X or order' and signing it, in which case X only may cash it. X can, however, endorse it again, either generally or specially, and the banker's draft may pass through several hands in this way. Usually, however, because the whole thing has been specifically arranged in advance, no endorsements are necessary.

Finally, the deposit has to be made over to you. If it has been held by estate agents as stakeholders, the buyer's solicitor must hand to you at completion a deposit release. This is a letter from him addressed to the estate agents saying, in effect: 'you may now pay the deposit to the seller, as the sale has now been completed'. Immediately after completion, you must write to the estate agents sending them the deposit release and asking them to send you a cheque for the deposit. In reply you should receive a cheque for the deposit, from which you will find that they have deducted their commission. Check that the commission is correctly calculated on the basis of the original agreement made with the estate agent.

If the deposit has been held in a joint account at a bank in the name of, say, the buyer's solicitor and yourself, then the buyer's solicitor should hand to you at completion a cheque already signed by him drawn on the joint account. You must then sign the cheque and pay it into your own account, and the joint account can then be closed.

The only other matter to arise at completion is giving possession of the house to the buyer. He is entitled to move in from the moment the sale is completed. The keys should therefore be handed to his solicitor at completion. Alternatively, they might be left with the estate agents, if this is more convenient. In this case, you should hand to the buyer's solicitor a letter addressed to the estate agents, authorising them to hand the keys to the buyer.

After completion, do not forget to cancel the insurance on the house. This does not usually apply in the case of a leasehold house, where the insurance is generally taken over by the buyer. Strictly speaking you might have cancelled the insurance as soon as contracts are exchanged, as the house was the buyer's responsibility from then on. But it is best to maintain the insurance until the money from the house is in your hands. And remember, too, to have the electricity and gas meters read on the day you move out, to notify the post office regarding the telephone and to cancel the instructions to your bank if you have been paying your building society by banker's order. These, however, are practical matters. The legal side, the part which involves solicitors, is over. With the money in the bank, the job is done.

APPROXIMATE COSTS ON THE TRANSFER OF PROPERTY—£10000 to £50000

Solicitors' scale fees for conveyancing were abolished from January 1973. Solicitors may charge whatever is "fair and reasonable". The list below is a guide to costs.

Cost of house £	Cost of building society valuation (buyer pays) £	Stamp duty on transfer (buyer pays) £	Land Registry fees on transfer (buyer pays) £	Solicitor's fee (including VAT) for acting for building society only (buyer pays) £
10000	21	nil	25·00	82·80
12500	26	nil	32·50	88·32
15000	31	nil	37·50	92·00
16250	33	81·25	42·50	94·94
17500	34	87·50	45·00	96·42
20000	36	100·00	50·00	99·36
22500	39	225·00	57·20	101·57
25000	41	250·00	62·00	104·88
27500	44	412·50	69·20	by arrangement
30000	46	450·00	74·00	by arrangement
35000	49	700·00	86·00	by arrangement
40000	51	800·00	98·00	by arrangement
45000	no set scale	900·00	110·00	by arrangement
50000	no set scale	1000·00	122·00	by arrangement

ABSTRACT OF TITLE: a summary of the important parts of the title deeds, by which a seller proves his ownership of a property which does not have a registered title. Also, in the case of a registered property, used—though not quite correctly—to describe the copy of the entries on the register, the filed plan and the authority to inspect the register.

ADMINISTRATORS: the personal representatives of a person who has died without a will or without appointing them executors in his will. They prove their authority by letters of administration issued by the High Court.

APPORTIONMENTS: the division between buyer and seller of liability for rates, water rates and other outgoings.

ASSENT: a document transferring a property from the personal representatives of a person who has died to the person now entitled to it.

ASSIGNMENT: a document which transfers from one person to another the ownership of property, such as an insurance policy or a leasehold house (unless it has a registered title, when it is called a transfer).

AUCTION: a sale, usually in public, to the highest bidder at the fall of the hammer. When a house is auctioned the buyer must sign a binding contract there and then. He should therefore have satisfied himself in advance by local searches, preliminary enquiries and a survey, that the house will be all it appears to be. The auction particulars should show whether the title to the house is registered.

AUTHORITY TO INSPECT THE REGISTER: the document, addressed to the Land Registry, by which the registered proprietor, that is the owner, allows someone else, usually the buyer's solicitor, to be given information about the register of a property, usually to enable him to make an official search.

BANKER'S DRAFT: a cheque signed by a bank manager, or one of his staff. As it is signed on behalf of the bank, instead of by the customer, it is almost inconceivable that it would not be met and is treated in practice as being equivalent to cash.

BENEFICIARY: the person who is entitled to the benefit of a property, in contrast with the person in whom the legal title only is vested, such as a trustee. In the case of a house, the beneficiary may obtain his benefit by receiving rent, or by living in it.

BRIDGING LOAN: a loan, usually from a bank, to tide a person over between the time when he has to pay the purchase price of one house and the time when the proceeds of sale of another and/or mortgage funds become available to him.

BUILDING SOCIETY: an organisation which specialises in lending money on mortgage to help people buy houses. Its funds come from money invested in the society by people who are paid interest.

CHARGE: any right or interest, subject to which freehold or leasehold property may be held, especially a mortgage; also used to denote a debit, or a claim for payment.

CHARGE CERTIFICATE: the certificate issued by the Land Registry to the mortgagee of a property which has a registered title, showing what is entered on the register of the property at the Land Registry. When there is no mortgage, a land certificate is issued instead to the registered proprietor.

CHARGEE: a person who can enforce a charge; a mortgagee.

CHARGES REGISTER: one of the three parts (the others are the property register and the proprietorship register) which go to make up the register at the Land Registry of a property with a registered title. The charges register contains details of restrictive covenants, mortgages and other interests, subject to which the registered proprietor owns the property.

CHATTELS: moveable possessions, such as furniture, clothes, jewellery and cars.

CHIEF RENT: a rentcharge; a sum periodically payable by an owner of a freehold property, in much the same way as ground rent is paid to a landlord by a leaseholder. Chief rents are usually for only a few pounds a year. They are payable for ever, and are more common in the north of England. They can be bought out by the freeholder compulsorily.

COMPLETION: the culmination of the procedure in the transfer of a house, when the necessary documents are handed over in exchange for the price.

COMPLETION STATEMENT: an account prepared by the seller, or his solicitor, setting out exactly how much money he claims should be paid by the buyer at completion, taking into account the price, the deposit and the apportionments.

COMPULSORY PURCHASE: the acquisition of property by a local authority, or other official body, whether or not the owner wishes to sell, under a power to do so contained in an act of parliament.

COMPULSORY REGISTRATION OF TITLE: the requirement in certain parts of England and Wales that any property, when next bought, should be registered at the Land Registry.

CONDITIONS OF SALE: the detailed standard terms which govern the rights and duties of the buyer and the seller of a house, as laid down in the contract which they sign. These may be the National or the Law Society's Conditions of Sale.

CONTRACT: any legally binding agreement; on the sale of a house this is the document, in two identical parts, one signed by the buyer and the other by the seller, which, when the parts are exchanged, commits both the buyer and the seller to complete the transaction by transferring ownership in exchange for paying the price.

CONVEYANCE: the deed by which the owner of a freehold property with an unregistered title transfers ownership of it to the buyer. If the property is leasehold, the deed is called an assignment and if the title is registered, the deed is called a transfer.

CONVEYANCING: that part of a solicitor's work which is concerned with the transfer of property and with rights and interests in connection with it.

COVENANT: a promise in a deed.

DEED: a legal document which, instead of being merely signed, is 'signed, sealed and delivered'. This can have a special significance; for example, a promise getting nothing in return is only enforceable in law if it is made in the form of a deed. The legal title to freehold and leasehold property can only be transferred by a deed.

DELIVERY: the handing over of a deed, after having been signed and sealed, with the intention that it should now be operative.

DEPOSIT: part of the purchase price, usually ten per cent, which the buyer pays on or before exchange of contracts. It is usually held by the seller's solicitor (sometimes a small part of it by the estate agent). It can be forfeited to the seller if the buyer withdraws after signing a binding contract.

DEPOSIT RELEASE: a letter signed by the buyer or his solicitor which permits the estate agents, if they hold a deposit, to hand it over to the seller, once the sale is completed.

DISCHARGE OF REGISTERED CHARGE: a document by which a building society, or other mortgagee, acknowledges that all the money secured by a mortgage on a registered property has been paid. It is usually made on the printed form known as form 53.

EASEMENT: a right which the owner of one property has over an adjoining property, such as a right of way or a right of light.

ENGROSSMENT: the actual deed or document which is executed or signed, as opposed to a mere draft of it.

ENQUIRIES BEFORE CONTRACT: a collection of detailed questions about many aspects of a property which the seller, or his solicitor, is generally asked to answer before the buyer is prepared to sign a contract. Also called preliminary enquiries.

ENQUIRIES OF LOCAL AUTHORITY: a number of questions asked of a local authority on a printed form about a particular property. The form is usually sent with, and loosely speaking forms part of, the buyer's local search.

ESTATE OWNER: the person in whom the legal ownership of a property is vested.

EXCHANGE OF CONTRACTS: the stage in the transfer of a house at which the buyer signs an engrossment of the contract and sends it to the seller, and the seller does the same in return, so that both become legally bound to go through with the transaction.

EXECUTE: to sign, seal and deliver a deed.

EXECUTORS: the personal representatives of a person who died leaving a will appointing them. They prove their entitlement by a grant of probate issued by the High Court.

FEE SIMPLE: freehold.

FILED PLAN: the Land Registry plan by reference to which a particular registered property is identified in the property register.

FIXTURES: articles, such as radiators, baths and tv aerials, which, because they are attached (by screws, concrete or pipes, for instance) to the house itself, as opposed to standing supported by their own weight, are presumed to have become legally part of the house itself, so that they are included in a sale, unless specifically excluded by the contract.

FORM 53: the form on which a mortgagee acknowledges that a mortgage of a property with a registered title has been paid off; the discharge of a registered charge.

FREEHOLD: the absolute ownership of property, as opposed to leasehold.

GOOD LEASEHOLD TITLE: the description given by the Land Registry to the title or ownership of a leasehold property having a registered title, where the Registry is entirely satisfied about the owner's entitlement to the lease itself, but has not enquired into the ownership of the freehold or other superior title of that property. In practice, good leasehold title is treated as being as good as title absolute.

GROUND RENT: the rent paid to the landlord by a leaseholder who owns a leasehold property. Ground rent for a house is often for not more than £20 a year, and the lease, when first granted, was for a long period, say 99 or even 999 years.

INTESTATE: having made no valid will.

JOINT TENANTS: two (or more) people who hold property jointly in such a way that, when one dies, the whole property automatically passes to the survivor. This is in contrast with what happens in the case of tenants in common.

LANDLORD: the person who is entitled to receive the rent from property which has been leased. It may be a long lease at a ground rent or one for a comparatively short period at a rack rent, or (occasionally) something between the two.

LAND CHARGES REGISTRY: a government department in Plymouth which keeps a register, open to public search, of certain charges on land in England and Wales the title to which is unregistered. It is quite distinct from the Land Registry, which deals only with properties where the title is registered.

LAND CERTIFICATE: the certificate issued to the registered proprietor of a property which has a registered title, showing what is entered on the register of that property at the Land Registry. When the property is mortgaged, no land certificate is issued and instead a charge certificate is issued to the mortgagee.

LAND REGISTRY: a government department whose head office is in London. District registries in various other places in England and Wales are responsible for opening maintaining and amending the registers of all properties in England and Wales which have registered titles. Not to be confused with the Land Charges Registry, which deals with properties which have unregistered titles.

LAW SOCIETY: the professional body governing solicitors. As well as looking after their interests, the Law Society maintains professional discipline over solicitors.

LAW SOCIETY'S CONDITIONS OF SALE: one of the available sets of standard terms which may be incorporated into a contract for the sale of a house and so govern the rights of the buyer and the seller; another such set is the National Conditions of Sale.

LEASEHOLD: ownership of property for a fixed number of years granted by a lease which sets out the obligations of the leaseholder, for example regarding payment of rent to the landlord, repairs and insurance; as opposed to freehold property, where ownership is absolute.

LEASEHOLDER: the person who, for the time being, owns a leasehold property. He can apply to the landlord to buy the freehold, and become the freeholder, if his lease is for more than 21 years.

LEGAL CHARGE: a mortgage, especially one framed so as to include the words 'legal charge'.

LESSEE: the person to whom a lease was originally granted, and, more commonly, the present leaseholder.

LESSOR: the person who originally granted a lease; also, the present landlord.

LETTERS OF ADMINISTRATION: the document issued by the High Court to administrators to prove that they have authority to act on behalf of a person who died without leaving a will appointing them to be executors.

LICENCE: permission to do something which, without it, would be illegal.

LICENCE TO ASSIGN: permission from a landlord allowing the leaseholder to transfer his lease to a specified person, as required by a clause in the lease.

LOCAL AUTHORITY: the local council responsible for roads, planning, social services and many other local matters on which rates are spent. All areas have two local authorities: a district council and a county council (or metropolitan district council and a metropolitan county council). In London there is the GLC and the borough councils.

LOCAL SEARCH: an application made on a special form to the local authority (the district council, or in London the borough council) for a certificate providing certain information about a property in the area. Also denotes the search certificate itself. A local search should reveal whether the property is likely to be affected by compulsory purchase, whether there are any outstanding sanitary notices, and similar matters. Loosely speaking, a local search also includes the answers given by the local authority to a number of standard additional enquiries, made on another special form; these answers are usually obtained at the time when the local search is made, but technically they are not part of it.

L.V.A. FORM: the form on which a buyer provides particulars of his purchase to the Inland Revenue. This is done immediately following completion. The form is also known as a PD ('Particulars Delivered') form and officially as Stamps L(A)451. It can be obtained from head post offices and Inland Revenue stamp offices. The initials L.V.A. stand for Land Valuation Act.

MAISONETTE: a flat, or any other separate dwelling, on more than one floor but forming only part of a building.

MORTGAGE (sometimes called a legal charge): a deed whereby freehold or leasehold property is pledged as security for a loan. It gives to the lender (such as a building society) certain rights in the property, including the power to sell if the mortgage payments are not made. These rights are cancelled when the money advanced is repaid with interest, in accordance with the agreed terms.

MORTGAGEE: one who lends money on mortgage, such as a building society, local authority, insurance company, bank or private lender.

MORTGAGOR: one who borrows money on mortgage, usually to enable him to buy a house.

NATIONAL CONDITIONS OF SALE: one of the available sets of standard terms which may be incorporated into a contract for the sale of a house, so as to govern the rights of the buyer and the seller of a property; another set is the Law Society's Conditions of Sale.

OFFICE COPY: an authenticated copy of an official document issued by the department or organisation which holds the original.

OFFICIAL SEARCH: an application to an official authority (such as a local authority, the Land Registry or the Land Charges Registry), to find out some relevant facts about a particular property.

OPTION MORTGAGE: a mortgage for borrowers who have little or no income tax liability. The borrower pays a lower rate of interest and in return foregoes entitlement to tax relief on mortgage interest. He can opt for the tax relief any time after four years, but has then to pay the normal interest rate.

OVERRIDING INTEREST: rights which are enforceable against a property, even though they are not referred to on the register of the property at the Land Registry; for instance, the right of a weekly tenant to remain in possession after the house has been sold, even though no mention of his tenancy is found on the register.

OYEZ: see Solicitors' Law Stationery Limited.

PERSONAL REPRESENTATIVES: the people who are authorised by a document issued by the High Court to represent the estate and interests of someone who has died. Where they were appointed by the will, they are called executors; where there is no will, or where the will did not specifically appoint them, they are called administrators.

PLANNING CONSENT OR PERMISSION: permission granted by a local authority under the Town and Country Planning Acts, to build on (or otherwise develop) property, or change its use.

POSSESSORY TITLE: the description given by the Land Registry to the title or ownership of a property where, due to some defect in the title, the registry is not entirely satisfied as to the owner's ownership of the property, but only satisfied that he is lawfully in possession of the property; as opposed to title absolute and good leasehold title.

PRELIMINARY ENQUIRIES: enquiries before contract.

PRIVATE TREATY: a contract not made at an auction.

PROBATE: the document issued by the High Court to executors to prove that they have authority under a will to act on behalf of someone who has died.

PROPERTY REGISTER: one of the three parts (the other two being the proprietorship register and the charges register) of the register of a property with a registered title. The property register sets out an exact description of the property concerned.

PROPRIETORSHIP REGISTER: one of the three parts (the other two being the property register and the charges register) of the register of a property with a registered title. The proprietorship register sets out the name and address of the registered proprietor, that is, the present owner, and the price which he paid for the property.

RACK RENT: a rent which represents more or less the full annual letting value of a property, as opposed to a ground rent (which is much smaller and is payable where a capital sum has been paid for the lease).

REAL PROPERTY: land, in particular freehold land, and any buildings on it, especially when used in the legal sense.

REGISTER: in the case of a property with a registered title, the record for that property kept at the Land Registry, divided into the property, the proprietorship and the charges registers.

REGISTERED PROPRIETOR: the person who is the owner of a property which has a registered title and is shown as such in the proprietorship register at the Land Registry.

REGISTERED TITLE: title or ownership of freehold or leasehold property which has been registered at the Land Registry, with the result that ownership is guaranteed by the state. In some parts of the country, registration of title is compulsory.

RENTCHARGE: a sum periodically payable by the owner of property under a covenant; a chief rent.

REQUISITIONS FOR AN OFFICIAL SEARCH: an application, on the appropriate form, for an official search.

REQUISITIONS ON TITLE: questions asked in writing by or on behalf of a buyer or mortgagee about matters concerning the seller's ownership of the property, and about other matters arising after exchange of contracts, as opposed to enquiries before contract.

RESTRICTIVE COVENANTS: obligations imposed by covenants on the owner of a freehold property, preventing him from doing certain things on his property, such as opening a business or putting buildings on certain parts of it.

RIGHT OF LIGHT: the right which an owner of a property sometimes has to prevent a neighbour from putting up a building or other obstruction which would to an unreasonable extent decrease the light to the owner's existing building; sometimes known as ancient lights.

RIGHT OF WAY: the right of an owner of a property (and those having his permission) to walk or drive over a neighbour's land.

ROAD CHARGES: the charges imposed on the owners of properties along a road, usually according to the frontage of each property, for the cost of making up or repairing the road.

ROOT OF TITLE: one of the title deeds, generally at least 15 years old, with which a seller starts his abstract of title, with the result that he undertakes to prove ownership from that time down to the present; applies only to properties with unregistered titles.

SCALE FEE: a fee calculated by reference to the price being paid, or money being borrowed, rather than to the amount of work involved. The scale fee for solicitors' conveyancing work was abolished in January 1973.

SEAL: a small paper disc stuck alongside the signature on a deed.

SEARCH: an enquiry for, or an inspection of, information recorded by some official authority, such as a local authority, the Land Registry or the Land Charges Registry.

SEARCH CERTIFICATE: the certificate of the result of a search.

SOLICITORS' LAW STATIONERY SOCIETY LIMITED: a company whose subsidiary, Oyez Publishing Ltd, publishes forms used in conveyancing. There are Oyez shops or sales offices in various parts of the country.

SOLICITOR'S UNDERTAKING: a letter signed by a solicitor in which he personally guarantees something, such as that his client's mortgage will be paid off. It is his professional duty to honour such an undertaking, even though he may suffer financially as a result if his client defaults.

STAKEHOLDER: one who holds a deposit as an intermediary between buyer and seller, so that the deposit may only be passed on to the seller with the permission of the buyer, or returned to the buyer with the permission of the seller.

STAMP DUTY: a duty payable to the government on some deeds and documents, including deeds of transfer, conveyance or assignment of property at a price above £15000. Deeds and documents cannot be used as evidence or registered at the Land Registry unless they are properly stamped.

SUBJECT TO CONTRACT: provisionally agreed, but not so as to constitute a binding legal contract. If the buyer and the seller have agreed terms 'subject to contract', either may still back out without giving any reason.

TENANT FOR LIFE: a beneficiary who is entitled to receive the rent or other income from property during his lifetime only, after which it will pass to others, in accordance with an existing will or trust.

TENANTS IN COMMON: two (or more) people who together hold property in such a way that, when one dies, his share does not pass automatically to the survivor but forms part of his own property and passes under his will or intestacy. This is in contrast with what happens in the case of joint tenants.

TITLE ABSOLUTE: the description given by the Land Registry to the title or ownership of a freehold (and sometimes leasehold) property where the registry is entirely satisfied about the owner's ownership of the property. Being registered with title absolute means that ownership is guaranteed by the state.

TITLE DEEDS: deeds and other documents which prove ownership of freehold or leasehold property. They normally consist of each deed transferring ownership over the previous fifteen years or more, together with mortgage deeds. Where the title is registered at the Land Registry, the title deeds are replaced by a land certificate, (or, if there is a mortgage, by a charge certificate) issued by the Land Registry.

TRANSFER: a deed which transfers the ownership of a freehold or leasehold property, the title to which is registered at the Land Registry (as opposed to the deed used where the title is unregistered, which is a conveyance in the case of a freehold, and an assignment in the case of a leasehold).

TRUSTEE: a person in whom the legal ownership of property is vested, but who holds it for the benefit of someone else (called a beneficiary), such as a child.

TRUSTEES FOR SALE: people who hold property as trustees on condition that they should sell the property, but usually with a power to postpone doing so indefinitely if they want to.

VENDOR: the seller.

Extending your house

describes what is involved in having an extension built on to a house or bungalow. The book is a step-by-step account of what has to be done, when and by whom. It deals with drawing a sketch plan, consulting an architect or other professional consultant, contacting a builder, arranging a contract and getting quotations. It explains how the Building Regulations affect the position and design of an extension, and how to apply to the local authority for planning permission and Building Regulations approval. For the technically-minded, various aspects of construction work are described. There is a glossary and many explanatory drawings.

Central heating

will help you to weigh up the alternative methods of heating your home. It discusses the factors you should consider when choosing the fuel, with charts of relative running costs. Finding an efficient installer, and dealing with him, are covered in detail, and so are the merits of various types of insulation. There is information, and illustrations, on all the equipment involved—boilers, radiators, circulation systems and methods of control. The book also gives advice on problems that might occur after installation.

Wills and probate

is a book about wills and how to make them and about the administration of an estate by executors without the help of a solicitor. It explains clearly about interpreting the will, the valuation of the estate, payment of estate duty, what is involved in obtaining probate, and the distribution of the estate. It also shows, with examples, how to prepare a will, sign it, and have it witnessed. The final section deals with intestacy.

What to do when someone dies

explains about doctors' certificates, about deaths reported to the coroner and what this entails, about registering a death and getting the various certificates that may be needed afterwards. Differences between burial and cremation procedure are discussed, and the arrangements that have to be made, mainly through the undertaker, for the funeral. The book details the various national insurance benefits that may be claimed.

Cutting your cost of living
suggests ways of spending less money without changing your standard of living. The book includes ideas on how to reduce your bills for food, toiletries, heating and holidays. There is a section on managing your money, and practical advice is given on growing your own fruit and vegetables, and on what jobs it is worth doing yourself.

How to sue in the county court
enables the consumer to sue in the county court, without a solicitor. It takes the layman step by step through what is involved and explains the procedure and rules. The letters he writes and receives, the information he has to get and give, the forms he has to complete, preparation for the trial, are all dealt with in detail. The book also deals with the important question of costs; how to make sure that you take your case to the right court; what to say in your particulars of claim; how to set about issuing a summons; what court fees are payable and settling out of court.

An ABC of motoring law
is a guide through the maze of criminal legislation which affects the motorist—in Scotland as well as England and Wales. It describes the offences you could commit, the people and procedures involved, and the penalties you could face. The book is arranged alphabetically, from alcohol to zigzag lines. Clear charts guide you through procedures such as reporting an accident or appearing in court.

Claiming on home, car and holiday insurance
gives a detailed account of the procedure for claiming on an insurance policy—notifying the insurers, filling in a claim form, providing evidence of the loss and its value, negotiations with the insurers, payment—and explains some of the terminology (excess, average, subrogation, reinstatement) and the people you may have to deal with, such as a broker, claims inspector, loss adjuster. Warnings are given about exclusions and conditions that may lead to a claim being turned down. The section on the home and possessions includes a table of examples of happenings for which you may want to claim on a policy and what you can expect to get.

Health for old age
sets out in plain language the minor and major physical changes that arise as people grow older, and the treatments available to relieve them. Advice is given about maintaining health, and about going to the doctor.

Living through middle age
faces up to the physical changes and psychological difficulties for both men and women that this stage of life may bring (some inevitable, and some avoidable). Throughout, practical advise is given on overcoming problems, so that you can make the most of your middle years.

Where to live after retirement
tackles the difficult subject of a suitable place to live in old age. The book offers practical advice on the decision whether to move or to stay put and adapt the present home to be easier to live in. It weighs up the pros and cons of the alternatives open to an older person, and the financial aspects involved, considers sheltered housing and granny flats, the problems of living in someone else's household, and residential homes.

Treatment and care in mental illness
deals briefly with the illnesses concerned and describes the help available through the national health service, from the local authority and from voluntary organisations. It explains the medical treatment a mentally ill person receives as an outpatient or an inpatient, and deals with community care and aftercare. It includes a chapter on the symptoms and treatment of mental illness in old age.

On getting divorced
explains the procedure for getting a divorce in England or Wales, and how, in a straightforward undefended case, it can be done by the postal procedure without paying for a solicitor. The legal advice scheme and other state help for someone with a low income is described and there is advice on coping in reduced circumstances. Calculations for maintenance and division of property are given, with details of the orders the court may make for financial settlements between the divorcing couple and for arrangements about the children.

Infertility
sets out what can and should happen in the systematic investigation of childlessness. It will not provide a ready answer to a couple's infertility, but it puts into perspective the physical factors associated with infertility (psychological factors can only be dealt with on a person-to-person level), and explains the medical and surgical treatment at present available.

Pregnancy month by month
goes in detail through what should happen when you are going to have a baby, mentioning some of the things that could go wrong and what can be done about them, and describing the available welfare services.

The newborn baby
concentrates primarily on health and welfare in the first few weeks after the baby is born, and also discusses feeding and development in the following months. There is advice about when to seek help from the midwife, health visitor, clinic doctor or general practitioner.

Which? way to slim
is a new comprehensive guide to the whole subject of slimming. Carefully sifting fact from fallacy, it sets out the best ways of going about losing weight and shows which method is most likely to suit which type of person. The book shows how to deal with possible danger times such as pregnancy, infancy and childhood, the teenage years and middle age. There are also sections on slimmers' cookery, foods and aids for slimmers, eating out, slimming groups, help from doctors, the psychology of slimming, activity and exercise. Tables of Calorie and carbohydrate values of foods and drinks are provided for easy day-to-day reference.

Having an operation
describes the procedure for admission to hospital and tells you what happens there: ward routine, hospital personnel, preparation for the operation, anaesthesia, post-operative treatment and recovery, and arrangements for discharge and convalescence. Basic information is given about some of the more common operations, explaining what is involved in the operation and any after-effects.

Earning money at home
is for the person who has to stay at home, and would like to make some money at the same time. The book explains what this entails in the way of organising domestic life, family and children, keeping accounts, taking out insurance, coping with tax, costing, dealing with customers, getting supplies. It suggests many activities that could be undertaken, with or without previous experience.

Avoiding back trouble

tells you about the spine and what can go wrong with the lower back. It deals with causes of back trouble, and gives hints on general care of the back when sitting, standing, lifting, carrying, doing housework and gardening. It describes how to cope with an attack of acute back pain, and discusses specialist examination and treatment, giving advice on how to avoid becoming a chronic sufferer and on exercises to strengthen and mobilise your spine.

Dismissal, redundancy and job hunting

for anyone who has been made redundant or (unfairly?) dismissed, the book explains the relevant legislation, minimum payments to which you may be entitled, how you can take your case to an industrial tribunal, how to claim unemployment benefit, what retraining opportunities there are, and how to set about looking for—and finding—another job.

In preparation: **a book about buying, selling and moving house.**

CONSUMER PUBLICATIONS are available from
Consumers' Association, Caxton Hill, Hertford SG13 7LZ
and from booksellers.